TALK

Italian

2

ALWENA LAMPING

Author and Series Editor

BBC Active, an imprint of Educational Publishers LLP, part of the Pearson Education Group, 80 Strand, London WC2R 0RL, England

First published 2007.
5

ISBN 978-1-4066-7916-8

Cover design: Two Associates
Cover photograph: © iStock.com/mrdoomits
Insides design: Nicolle Thomas, Rob Lian
Layout: Rob Lian
Illustrations © Tim Marrs @ Central Illustration Agency
Commissioning editor: Debbie Marshall
Development editor: Sarah Boas
Project editor: Melanie Kramers
Marketing: Fiona Griffiths, Paul East
Senior production controller: Man Fai Lau

Audio producer: Martin Williamson, Prolingua Productions
Sound engineer: Dave Morritt at Studio AVP
Presenters: Benedetta Ferraro, Jessica Juffre, Aldo Alessio, Matteo Ghilardi

Printed and bound in China. (CTPSC/05)

The Publisher's policy is to use paper manufactured from sustainable forests.

Contents

Introduction

Talk Italian 2 is a new course from BBC Active, helping you to improve your Italian in an enjoyable and stimulating way. It's designed for people who have some experience of Italian – whether from an introductory course (such as the bestselling **Talk Italian**), a first-level class or time spent in Italy – and who want to build on what they've learnt.

Recognising that language is reinforced through repetition, **Talk Italian 2** takes time to revisit the basics, as well as taking you forward at a sensible and manageable pace. The course deals with interesting, adult topics such as food and wine, getting to know people, finding out about Italian property, shopping and coping with problems. It's ideal, whether you want to learn for work or for fun, and as preparation for a national Level 1 qualification. Free tutors' support and activities are available at www.bbcactivelanguages.com/TeachersHome/ResourcesItalian.aspx

What makes **Talk Italian 2** special?
- It has been developed by a team of professionals with extensive experience in adult language learning.
- The carefully designed activities focus on all the dimensions of learning Italian and aim to develop your ability to speak the language, understand replies, and experiment with reading and writing in Italian.
- It recognises that, in order to go beyond basic phrases and really express yourself, you'll need to know some Italian grammar. And it presents the grammar in a way that's easy to understand, without jargon or complex technical explanations.
- It incorporates highly effective learning strategies, such as predicting, educated guesswork, memory building, gist reading and selective use of a glossary.
- Its structured and systematic approach promotes steady progress and a real sense of achievement, boosting your confidence as well as your linguistic ability.

Talk Italian 2, which includes this book and 140 minutes of audio recordings by native Italian speakers, is an interactive course, involving you at all the stages of the learning process.

Wherever you see this: **1•5**, the phrases or dialogues are recorded on the CD (i.e. CD1, track 5).

It consists of:

Units 1 to 10, each containing:

- *In Italia*, an insight into Italian culture to set your learning in context;
- summaries of key language for you to listen to, read and repeat to practise your pronunciation;
- activities designed around the audio recordings, to develop your listening skills and understanding;
- succinct *In italiano* explanations of how the language works, placed exactly where you need the information (where appropriate, these are expanded in the grammar section at the back - see links e.g. **G15**);
- a *Put it all together* section, consolidating what you've learnt before you put it to the test in *Now you're talking*, where you are prompted to speak Italian;
- a final progress check with a quiz and a checklist summarising key points.

In più supplements, at regular intervals, which will:

- take you that little bit further, reinforcing and extending what you've learnt in the two preceding units;
- broaden your vocabulary and/or place words that you know into a new context;
- develop your reading and writing skills.

A comprehensive reference section:

- a set of clear definitions of essential grammar terms (on page 6)
- transcripts of all the audio material
- answers to the activities
- a guide to pronunciation and spelling
- a grammar section
- Italian-English glossary
- English-Italian glossary.

BBC Active would like to thank all the language tutors who contributed to the planning of the **Talk 2** series. Our particular thanks go to Pam Lander Brinkley MA (Ed), Sue Maitland, York ACES (Adult and Community Education Service) and Liviana Ferrari.

Glossary of grammatical terms

To make the most of the *In italiano* notes, it helps to know the meaning of the following key grammatical terms.

- **Nouns** are the words for people, places, concepts and things: *son, doctor, sheep, house, Scotland, time, freedom*.
- **Gender** Every Italian noun is either masculine or feminine, as are any articles and adjectives that relate to it.
- **Articles** are *the* (definite article) and *a/an* (indefinite article).
- **Pronouns** avoid the need to repeat nouns: *it, them, you, they*.
- **Singular** means one.
- **Plural** means more than one.
- **Adjectives** describe nouns: *Italian* wine, the children are *small*.
- **Adverbs** add information to adjectives and verbs: *very* big, to speak *slowly*.
- **Verbs** are words like *to go, to sleep, to eat, to like, to have, to be*, that refer to doing and being.
- **Infinitive** Italian verbs are listed in a dictionary in the infinitive form, ending in **-are**, **-ere** or **-ire**. The English equivalent is *to*: *to eat, to have*.
- **Regular verbs** follow a predictable pattern, while **irregular verbs** don't – they have to be learnt separately.
- The **person** of a verb indicates who or what is doing something:

  1st person = the speaker: *I* (singular), *we* (plural)
  2nd person = the person(s) being addressed: *you*
  3rd person = who/what is being talked about: *he/she/it/they*

- The **tense** of a verb indicates when something is done:

in the past	perfect tense	*I worked, I have worked*
	imperfect tense	*I was working, I used to work*
now	present tense	*I work, I'm working*
in the future	future tense	*I will work*

- The **subject** of a sentence is the person/thing carrying out the verb: *they* have two children, *Anna* reads the paper.
- The **object** of a sentence is at the receiving end of a verb: they have *two children*, Anna reads *the paper*.

Vado pazzo per l'Italia

getting to know people

giving information about people

talking about work

explaining why you're learning Italian

In Italia ...

a popular way of learning Italian is to combine **un corso d'italiano** with **un'esperienza culturale**, and if you search on the Internet for **soggiorno linguistico** *language holiday*, you'll come across all sorts of options. You can discover **agriturismo** *rural tourism* while learning to cook or observing **la natura**, find out about **la musica** or **la storia dell'arte** *art history* in one of Italy's glorious cities or throw yourself into **sport e avventura** ... all the while improving your Italian in the company of like-minded people from various parts of the world.

Getting to know people

1 1•2 Listen to the key language:

Come ti chiami?	What's your name?
Mi chiamo ...	My name is ...
Di dove sei?	Where are you from?
Sono di ...	I'm from ...
Dove abiti?	Where do you live?
Abito in Italia/a Roma.	I live in Italy/in Rome.

2 1•3 At the start of a **corso di lingua e cucina italiana** in Umbria, the teacher, rather than introduce herself, invites people to ask her some questions. She opens with **Diamoci del tu** *Let's use 'tu'.* Listen and make a note of her first name and where she lives.

Nome .... *Baldoni*   **Domicilio** ....

3 1•4 Jack and Angelika, two of the people on the course, are getting to know each other. Listen and fill the gaps in their conversation.

- Ciao, ... chiamo Jack.
- Piacere Jack. ...... inglese? Americano?
- ...... irlandese. Tu, come ...... chiami?
- Angelika.
- Di dove ...... ?
- Sono ...... Lodz in Polonia, sono polacca. Ma ...... in Germania.
- E io abito ...... Inghilterra, vicino ...... Bristol, con mio fratello.

4 Have a go at introducing yourself, giving your name and nationality and saying where you live.

In italiano

In a more formal setting, **lei** would be used instead of **tu**:

sei	abiti	ti chiami	would become
è	abita	si chiama	

because **lei** uses the 3rd person singular form of a verb, the same form as 'he' and 'she'.   **G14**

Giving information about people

1 **1•5** Listen to the key language:

Vi presento ...	Let me introduce ... to you (all).
Si chiama ...	His/Her name is ...
Si chiamano ...	Their names are ...
Abita ..., Abitano ...	He/She lives ..., They live ...
È ...	He/She is ...
Hai ...	You have ... (**tu**)
Ha ...	You have ... (**lei**), He/She has ...

2 **1•6** Jack and Angelika have been asked to introduce each other to the rest of the group. Have another look at their conversation on page 8 and see if you could introduce them, then listen to how they do it and compare the two. *His brother* is **suo fratello**.

The ending of a verb changes from the infinitive ending -are, -ere, -ire, depending on who/what is involved. For most verbs the endings are regular and predictable:

	-are	-ere	-ire
io *I*	-o	-o	-(isc)o
tu *you*	-i	-i	-(isc)i
lui *he*, lei *she/you*	-a	-e	-(isc)e
noi *we*	-iamo	-iamo	-iamo
voi *you*	-ate	-ete	-ite
loro *they*	-ano	-ono	-(isc)ono

In italiano

G15

3 **1•7** Lucia's students ask more questions. Listen, then decide whether the following facts about her are true or false. **Sua figlia** is *her daughter*.

		vero	falso
a	Lucia è sposata.		
b	Suo marito si chiama Luca.		
c	Hanno quattro figli.		
d	Sua figlia si chiama Lucia.		
e	Sua figlia ha quattordici anni.		

Now write the correct version of any that are false. You might need the transcript on page 107.

Talking about work

1 **1•8** Listen to the key language:

Che lavoro fai?	What do you do?
Lavoro in/per ...	I work in/for ...
Sono ...	I'm a/an ...
Faccio il/la ...	I'm a/an ...
Da quanto tempo?	Since when?/How long for?
Dal 2003./Da cinque anni.	Since 2003./For five years.

2 **1•9** Match the Italian words to the illustrations, using the glossary if you need to. Then listen to people talking about what they do for a living and tick the occupations you hear mentioned.

☐ **infermiere/infermiera**
☐ **cameriere/cameriera**
☐ **organizzatore/organizzatrice di escursioni**
☐ **illustratore/illustratrice**
☐ **programmatore/programmatrice**
☐ **idraulico (m/f)**

To say you've been doing something for a period of time or since a particular time, you use **da** and the present tense.

Abito qui da febbraio. *I've been living here since February.*
Studio ... da un anno. *I've been learning ... for a year.*
Da becomes **dal** before a year:
Lavoro ... dal 2005. *I've been working ... since 2005.*   **G15**

3 **1•10** Listen to Danie and Marc talking about what they do and underline the correct information.

a Danie has been working as a press officer for the government since 2000 / 2002 / 2003.

b Marc has been an estate agent for 3 / 13 / 30 years.

Explaining why you're learning Italian

1   **1•11** Listen to the key language:

Perché ...	Why?/ Because ...
Mi piace ...	I like ...
... viaggiare/l'Italia.	... travelling/Italy.
Mi piacciono le lingue.	I like languages.
Vorrei ...	I'd like to ...
Vado pazzo per ...	I'm crazy about ...

2   **1•12** Lucia asks people why they want to learn Italian: **Perché vuoi imparare l'italiano?** Here's how they reply.

First of all, match the Italian and the English, then listen and tick the replies as you hear them. Which one was not mentioned?

a	Mi piace la cultura italiana.	1	I like Italian food and wines.
b	Mi piacciono le lingue.	2	I like languages.
c	Vado pazzo per l'Italia.	3	Out of curiosity – that's all!
d	Vorrei lavorare in Italia.	4	I really like travelling.
e	Mi piace molto viaggiare.	5	I'd like to work in Italy.
f	Per comunicare con la fidanzata di mio figlio.	6	I like Italian culture.
g	Per curiosità – e basta!	7	Opera's my passion.
h	La musica lirica è la mia passione.	8	I'm crazy about Italy.
i	Mi piacciono la cucina e i vini italiani.	9	To communicate with my son's fiancée.

3   **1•13** Anna's learning because her son's marrying an Italian girl. Listen and see if you can pick out where her future **nuora** *daughter-in-law* is from and what her name is.

Nome ....   **Città** ....

4   Using a dictionary if necessary, work out how to say why you're learning Italian.

put it **all together**

1 Match the Italian and the English.

a Mi piacciono i vini italiani.	**1** I like working in Italy.
b Come si chiama?	**2** I like Italian wine.
c Vorrei lavorare in Italia.	**3** How long for?
d Mi piace il vino italiano.	**4** What are their names?
e Mi piace lavorare in Italia.	**5** I'd like to work in Italy.
f Come si chiamano?	**6** What's her name?
g Da quanto tempo?	**7** I like Italian wines.

2 Change the ending of **parlare** *to speak*, **leggere** *to read* and **dormire** *to sleep* to agree with **io**, **tu**, **lei** and **loro**. Even though you might not yet have come across them, you should still be able to predict the endings.

	io	tu	lei	loro
parlare				
leggere				
dormire				

3 Here's a profile of a graphic designer from Naples.

Cognome Gallo
Nome Roberto
Data di nascita
3 dicembre 1975
Nazionalità Italiano
Roberto Gallo
Domicilio Napoli   **Da** 15 anni
Professione grafico   **Da** 8 anni

a How might he introduce himself, giving his name, age in 2007 and nationality; and saying where he lives and works and how long he's been living there and doing this work?
b And how would you introduce him to a group of people? *He's a designer* is **Fa il grafico**.

4 Now think of two people you know and practise introducing them to others.

now you're talking!

1 **1•14** You're going to be asked these questions. Answer them as if you were Rachel Cavanagh, who's been working as a scientist for the past seven years. She's learning Italian because she likes travelling and fancies working in Italy.

- **Ciao! Come ti chiami?**
- **Sei americana, vero?**
- **Di dove sei in Inghilterra?**
- **Che lavoro fai?**
- **Da quanto tempo sei scienziata?**
- **Perché vuoi imparare l'italiano?**

Cognome Cavanagh
Nome Rachel
Nazionalità Inglese
Domicilio
Cambridge, Inghilterra
Professione
Scienziata

Rachel Cavanagh

2 **1•15** Now it's your turn to ask the questions. You're in a queue with someone about your age and you start a conversation by saying *Hi* and asking what his name is.

- **Lorenzo – Lorenzo Bruno. Piacere.**
- ◆ Ask Lorenzo where he's from.
- **Sono di Milano.**
- ◆ Find out whether he's living in Milan.
- **No. Abito a Perugia da tre anni ... dal duemilaquattro quando mi sono sposato.**
- ◆ Ask what he does for a living.
- **Sono grafico. Lavoro da casa perché ho una bambina piccola.**
- ◆ Ask how old she is.
- **Ha quattordici mesi. È proprio bellina.**

quiz

1 If someone says **Diamoci del tu**, what are they suggesting?

2 How would you introduce Giorgio to a group of people?

3 When you're talking about yourself, what letter does the verb generally end in?

4 To say your son is 12, do you need **ho**, **hai** or **ha** in the gap? **Mio figlio** ...... **dodici anni**.

5 What's the Italian for Poland?

6 If you've been working in York since 1998, what word will you need to insert here? **Lavoro a York** ...... **1998**.

7 Would you use **mi piace** or **mi piacciono** to say you like travelling?

8 What is **la musica lirica**?

Now check whether you can ...

- introduce yourself
- say where you live and what you do for a living
- say how long you've been doing these
- explain why you're learning Italian
- ask people their names, what they do and where they live
- introduce someone
- provide information about where they live and work

Successful language learning needs plenty of practice and it also helps to have a personal angle – it's much easier to remember words that have an immediate relevance to you personally. So, using a dictionary, start to boost your vocabulary by creating as many sentences as you can starting with **Sono**, **Mi piace/piacciono**, **Non mi piace/piacciono**, **Vado pazzo per**.

Alle otto e mezzo

using the 24-hour clock

... and the 12-hour clock

talking about daily routine

... and the working day

In Italia ...

although the 24-hour clock is widely used in formal situations such as timetables or business appointments, you'll also come across the 12-hour clock in informal everyday speech. It's simple to recognise: **e** for minutes past the hour and **meno** for minutes to the hour, for example **le nove** *nine o'clock*, **le nove e un quarto** *quarter past nine*, **le nove e mezzo** *half past nine*, **le nove meno venti** *twenty to nine*. **Di mattina/pomeriggio/sera** *in the morning/afternoon/evening* are used if clarification is needed: **alle cinque e mezzo di mattina** *at five thirty in the morning*.

Using the 24-hour clock

1   1•17 Listen to the key language:

Comunque ...	However ...
C'è un volo che parte alle ...	There's a flight that leaves at ...
Il prossimo parte alle ...	The next one leaves at ...
Il mio volo arriva alle ...	My flight arrives at ...
C'è un volo prima delle ...?	Is there a flight before ...?

2   1•18 En route from Lisbon to Bari, Jorge Chavez misses his connection in Rome. Listen to the information he's given at check-in, and make a note of what time the next three flights leave, even though the first is **pieno** *full*, with no seat available.

- **C'è un volo per Bari che parte alle** ...... **Comunque è pieno, non c'è nessun posto disponibile.**
- ◆ **E il prossimo volo?**
- **Il prossimo parte alle** ...... **e ce n'è un altro alle** ....
- ◆ **Non c'è un volo prima delle** ......?

In italiano

> When **a**, **di** or **da** come before **le**, they combine with it:
> **alle nove** *at nine o'clock*   **prima delle nove** *before nine o'clock*
> **dalle nove alle undici** *from nine till eleven o'clock*
> The exceptions are *one o'clock*, *midday* and *midnight*:
> **all'una, prima di mezzogiorno, da mezzanotte.**   **G4**

3   1•19 Jorge's in Italy for a **convegno** *conference*. Listen as he rings Alessandro Pardo, a colleague, and leaves him a message. What time does he say his flight will be arriving?

4   At the last minute, the airline got Jorge on the earlier flight. How will he let Alessandro know that he'll be arriving at 6.25pm?

Scusi per la confusione, ma ....

5   1•20 Jorge receives this message from Alessandro, asking him to call him from Bari airport. What are the missing words? Listen to check.

Signor Chavez, ho appuntamenti .... 16.00 .... 18.30.
Mi chiami dall'aeroporto di Bari. A più tardi.

... and the 12-hour clock

6   **1•21** Listen to the key language:

alle dieci e un quarto	at a quarter past ten
alle dieci e mezzo	at half past ten
alle undici meno un quarto	at a quarter to eleven
fino alle sette di sera	until seven in the evening

In the 1st person plural, i.e. with **noi** *we*, verbs end in *-iamo*:

cominciare *to start*	**cominciamo** *we start*
riprendere *to resume*	**riprendiamo** *we resume*
riunirsi *to meet up*	**ci riuniamo** *we meet up*
fare una pausa *to have a break*	**facciamo una pausa** *we have a break*

G15

In italiano

---

7   **1•22** Later, Alessandro tells Jorge about the first day of the conference. Listen, then fill the gaps with the **noi** form of the verbs in the box below, in the order you find them. Listen again.

> ## IL CAMBIAMENTO CLIMATICO
> rischio per la biodiversità marina
> CONVEGNO EUROPEO 17-19 aprile

.... **alle dieci e un quarto con il discorso del Ministro sul cambiamento climatico.**

Alle undici meno un quarto .... **gli altri delegati europei e** .... **informazioni. Alle undici e mezzo** .... **una pausa per il caffè, poi** .... **fino al pranzo all'una.**

Dopo pranzo, c'è un po' di relax fino alle sette di sera quando ci riuniamo per l'aperitivo. .... **insieme alle otto e mezzo.**

cominciare *to start*	**incontrare** *to meet*	**scambiare** *to exchange*
fare *to make/do/have*	**riprendere** *to resume*	**cenare** *to have dinner*

Talking about daily routine

1   1•23 Listen to the key language:

di solito/qualche volta	usually/sometimes
Mi sveglio ...	I wake up ...
Mi alzo ...	I get up ...
... presto/tardi.	... early/late.
Mi alleno in palestra.	I train in the gym.
Mi faccio la doccia.	I have a shower.
Vado/Andiamo a letto.	I go/We go to bed.

2   1•24 As you listen to six people talking about their morning routine, jot down whether they wake up or get up at these times.

a `07.00`   c `08.00`   e `08.50`

b `07.30`   d `06.45`   f `06.30`

In italiano

The infinitive of some verbs ends in **-si**: **alzarsi** *to get up*, **chiamarsi** *to be called*, **riunirsi** *to get together*.
The **si** changes to **mi**, **ti**, **si**, **ci** or **vi**, depending on who is involved, and goes before the verb:

mi alzo *I get up*	ci alziamo *we get up*
ti alzi *you get up*	vi alzate *you (pl) get up*
si alza *he/she gets up*	si alzano *they get up*

G26

3   1•25 Listen to Alessandro telling Jorge about his daily routine and see if you can catch:

a   what time he normally gets up;
b   what he does after work – and where he does it;
c   what he does after this.

Now say what time you normally wake up and get up.

... and the working day

4   **1•26** Listen to the key language:

A che ora ...?	What time ...?
Alessandro fa il pendolare.	Alessandro commutes.
Monica non fa la pendolare.	Monica doesn't commute.
Lavora a/da casa.	He/She works at/from home.
Vado ... , Va ...	I go..., He/She goes ...
Esco..., Esce ...	I go out ..., He/She goes out ...

5   **1•27** Listen as Alessandro's wife Monica talks about their routine, and tick whether these statements apply to Monica, Alessandro or to both.

	M	A
Mi sveglio presto.		
Mi alzo alle 8.		
Mi alzo alle 7.		
Lavoro da casa.		
Sono web designer.		
Faccio il pendolare.		

	M	A
Esco di casa alle 7.25.		
Vado in palestra la sera.		
Mi alleno.		
Torno a casa.		
Ceno alle 20.15.		

In italiano

There are some verbs that don't follow the regular patterns:

	io	lui/lei	noi	loro
andare *to go*	vado	va	andiamo	vanno
avere *to have*	ho	ha	abbiamo	hanno
essere *to be*	sono	è	siamo	sono
fare *to make*	faccio	fa	facciamo	fanno
uscire *to go out*	esco	esce	usciamo	escono

These irregular verbs have to be learned individually. There's a full list of these and other common ones on page 136.   **G16**

6   Can you:

- ask a friend what time he/she wakes up and gets up?
- say what time someone you know wakes up and gets up?
- say these things about yourself and another person, using *we*?

put it all together

1 Find a connection between the words in the two columns.

a	cenare	1	discorso
b	allenarsi	2	pausa
c	uscire	3	treno
d	svegliarsi	4	sera
e	caffè	5	palestra
f	convegno	6	mattina
g	pendolare	7	esco

2 Write the following in Italian, in 12-hour clock format.

a at **07.30**   **alle sette e mezzo di mattina**

b at **20.00**   d at **06.20**

c at **16.15**   e at **23.00**

3 Fill the gaps with the right form of the verb.

a **Salvatore è architetto.** .... **a Bergamo.** (lavorare)
b **Il convegno non** .... **presto.** (cominciare)
c **Mia moglie ed io** .... **da casa.** (lavorare)
d **Sabato, noi** .... **alle nove e mezzo.** (alzarsi)
e **Dopo il lavoro, io** .... **in palestra.** (allenarsi)
f **Io** .... **alle sette.** (alzarsi)

4 How would you tell someone in Italian that you

- normally wake up early
- then (**poi**) get up at 7.30
- leave the house at eight o'clock
- and go to work
- get back home at seven o'clock in the evening
- read the paper or watch television (**guardare la televisione**)
- have supper
- sometimes go to bed at eleven o'clock?

now you're talking!

1   **1•28** Answer these questions as if you are Dan Perrett, a
    database administrator from the north-west of England.

- ● **Dan, dove abiti?**
- ◆ Say you live in Cheshire (use **nel** for *in*).
- ● **Ma lavori a Manchester, vero?**
- ◆ Say yes, you commute.
- ● **Di solito a che ora ti alzi?**
- ◆ Say you normally wake up at seven o'clock and get up at
  ten past.
- ● **E a che ora esci di casa?**
- ◆ Say you leave at half past seven.

2   **1•29** Now answer the questions as if you are Dan's wife, Sarah,
    a GP. You'll notice that two of the verbs in the questions end in
    -ate. That's because they refer to both Dan and Sarah.

- ● **Sarah, a che ora si alza Dan?**
- ◆ Say he gets up at ten past seven.
- ● **Dove lavora?**
- ◆ Say he works in Manchester and leaves the house at
  half past seven.
- ● **Sarah, ti piace l'aerobica, vero?**
- ◆ Say yes, you train in the gym.
- ● **La sera, mangiate insieme?**
- ◆ **Insieme** means *together*. Say yes, you eat together
  at home.
- ● **A che ora cenate?**
- ◆ Say you usually eat at seven in the evening.

quiz

1   What time is **le quattro meno venticinque di pomeriggio**?

2   Is **tardi** or **presto** the Italian for *early*?

3   What's **cambiamento climatico**?

4   Add **sessanta** and **dodici**. What's the answer in Italian?

5   Is it **mi**, **si** or **ci** that's missing here? ...... **alziamo alle nove.**

6   If *to leave* is **partire** and *to arrive* is **arrivare**, how would you say *we leave at half past five and arrive at seven o'clock*?

7   *Marta commutes* is **Marta** ....

8   What's the connection between **esce** and **usciamo**?

Now check whether you can ...

- understand and say times using both the 12- and 24-hour clock
- say what happens when
- say *we* do something if you're given the infinitive of a verb
- talk about your daily routine
- describe people's work routine

This first section of *Talk Italian 2* has been about revisiting the basics as well as extending your Italian. There's more consolidation to come in **In più** but, if you're finding at this stage that some of what you learnt previously has escaped your memory, now would be a good time to remind yourself of numbers (see page 131), vocabulary and key basics. It can be quite therapeutic to go over something familiar that you learnt very early on.

In più 1

Verb endings are crucially important because words like io, tu, lui, lei, noi are generally included only for emphasis or contrast. For the great majority of verbs, the endings follow a regular pattern, with minor variations depending on whether the infinitive ends in -are, -ere or -ire.

G15

1 Simona and Enzo, school friends who haven't met for years, bump into each other in Bologna. Read their conversation and add the ending to the verbs. If you need to refresh your memory before you start, there's a table of endings on page 9.

> Sei tu Simona?

> Enzo! È da tanto tempo che non ci vediamo!
> *It's such a long time since we've seen each other.*

S Dove abit...... adesso?

E Qui a Bologna, da quasi tre mesi. Abit...... in via Savanella.
I miei genitori abit...... in periferia come sempre.

S Anche tua sorella Laura abit...... in Emilia-Romagna, vero?

E Sì, sì. Lei e Stefano abit...... a Sant'Agata, fra Bologna e Modena.

S Stefano lavor...... al museo Lamborghini?

E No, è studente. Frequent...... l'Università di Bologna; segu......
un corso di Scienze della Comunicazione.
Parl...... tre lingue: italiano, inglese e un po' di giapponese.

S E tu, dove lavor......?

E A Modena. Faccio il pendolare; mi alz...... alle sei e mezzo e
prend...... il treno delle sette. Che incubo! Ma ogni tanto, quando
lavor...... da casa, mi alz...... alle dieci! Anche mia moglie si
alz...... presto perché i bambini si svegli...... alle sei ogni giorno.

S Tu hai bambini?! Come si chiam......?

frequentare *to attend*	**prendere** *to catch*	**seguire** *to follow*
un incubo *a nightmare*	**i miei genitori** *my parents*	
ogni *every*	**ogni tanto** *every so often*	

2 Using the 12-hour clock, how would you tell a visitor to the UK what time banks and shops usually open and close?

Nel Regno Unito	le banche	aprono alle
	i negozi	chiudono alle

When talking about going to or being in a place, you use:

- a with cities, towns or villages: **a Roma**, **a Monza**, **a Montalcino**.
- in with continents, countries and regions: **in Asia**, **in Brasile**, **in Irlanda**, **in Abruzzo**, **in Sicilia**, **in Toscana**, **in Umbria**.
- in + definite article for the UK, **nel Regno Unito**, and for UK counties: **nel Kent**, **nel Cheshire**.
- in + definite article for places with a plural name: **nei Paesi Bassi**, **negli Stati Uniti**, **nelle Canarie**, **nelle Maldive**.

G3

3 Following the word order of these examples, make up at least 12 new sentences, each mentioning a different person/persons and a different place.

Mio fratello	lavora	in	Arabia Saudita
I miei genitori	abitano	nel	Regno Unito
Io	vado	nelle	Maldive
nome	va	in	Turchia
Noi	andiamo	a	Londra

4 How quickly can you unscramble these member states of the **Unione Europea (l'UE)**? How would you say you're going to these countries?

a OBLIGE

b RAINDAL

c LOGOPATROL

d DILFANIAN

e CARGIE

f ATONISE

5 Read what Lucia's nine-year-old son Marco produced in school when asked to write about his family. Try to get the gist without using the glossary. **Vivere** is another word for *to live*.

> ### La mia famiglia di Marco Baldoni
>
> Vi presento la mia famiglia.
>
> Il mio bisnonno si chiama Giuseppe Baldoni e ha settantacinque anni. Nato nel 1932, prima della Seconda Guerra Mondiale, è molto molto vecchio. È vedovo e vive da solo.
>
> Suo figlio Roberto è mio nonno. Anche lui è vecchio. È sposato con mia nonna Sofia che ha cinque sorelle. Povera nonna, io ho soltanto una sorella che ha quattro anni e si chiama Laura.
>
> I miei nonni hanno tre figli, due maschi e una femmina. Mio zio Giovanni, il più grande, lavora da molti anni in Brasile. Fa il banchiere (penso). Ho tre cugini in Brasile. Vivono in una casa grande a São Paulo.
>
> Poi c'è mio padre Luciano che è sposato con mia mamma. Mia mamma si chiama Lucia Baldoni. Sua madre, nonna Paola, vive in Veneto. Noi andiamo in Veneto qualche volta.
>
> Anche mia zia Marta vive lontano. Dal 2005 abita negli Stati Uniti con zio Pietro e le mie cugine che si chiamano Carla e Fiorella. Non mi piace molto Fiorella. FINE

Choose the right option. You'll probably need to use the glossary for this, and it might even help to sketch out a family tree.

a Giovanni è il nonno / padre / fratello / cognato di Marta.
b Paola è la sorella / madre / cugina / suocera di Luciano.
c Marco è il figlio / fratello / cugino / nipote di Roberto.
d Marco ha tre / quattro / cinque / sei cugini.
e Il suocero di Sofia si chiama Roberto / Marco / Giuseppe / Pietro.
f Il nonno di Giovanni si chiama Roberto / Marco / Giuseppe / Pietro.
g I genitori di Luciano hanno due / tre / quattro / cinque figli.
h Carla e Fiorella sono cugine / zie / sorelle / nonne.

6 Jorge Chavez is in Bari for the **Cambiamento Climatico** conference and will be introducing himself to the other delegates.
Write down what he might say, based on this information.

Nationality: Portuguese   Works in: Lisbon
Profession: Scientist
Has worked for the **Centro Conservazione** since 2001
Languages spoken: Portuguese, Spanish, Italian, English

After the conference, a few delegates meet informally. Write down how Jorge would tell them he
- lives in Cascais in Portugal and commutes to work,
- has been married for two years and has a son,
- really likes travelling and would like to work in Brazil.

7 How would you say what these people do and how long they've been doing it? The first two are done for you.

 a Giorgio, seven years
Giorgio è postino
da sette anni.

 b Marta, 2002
Marta è dentista
dal 2002.

 c Nico, 2001

 e Francesca, three years

 d Ornella, one year

 f Valter, 2005

Si può prenotare qui?

getting local information

... and advice

talking about leisure interests

planning an activity

In Italia ...

not only are there so many historic and artistic treasures that the country has been described as **una galleria d'arte all'aperto** *open-air art gallery*, but it also boasts 18 **Parchi Nazionali** and 89 **Parchi Regionali**. **ENIT** – the Italian National Tourist Board – provides information about things to see and do both online and in local **APT (Azienda di Promozione Turistica)** offices. Events and activities on offer range from **sagre** *food and wine festivals* to **sport**, including **sport estremi** *extreme sports* such as **parapendio** *paragliding* or **rafting** *white-water rafting*. And, with 7,600 kilometres of coastline, there's no shortage of **spiagge** *beaches* and **sport nautici** *water sports*.

Getting local information

1 **1•30** Listen to the key language:

C'è/Ci sono ... qui vicino?	Is/Are there ... round here?
Ce ne sono tanti.	There are so many of them.
Posso ..., Possiamo ...?	Can I ..., Can we ...?
Puoi ...?	Can you ...? (**tu**)
Si può ...?	Can one .../Is it possible to ...?

2 **Informazioni turistiche** publications such as the following are freely available in Italian tourist offices. See if you can work out what these are: many of the words are similar to English words, so only use the glossary if you're really stuck. **Elenco** and **lista** both mean list.

Guida Enogastronomia

Piantina della città

Guida Sport e Avventura

Guida Agriturismo

Cartina della regione

Lista campeggi

Elenco ristoranti

Orario apertura del museo

Lista Escursioni Guidate

Calendario Eventi e Spettacoli

3 **1•31** Listen to people making enquiries at the **APT**. Which of the above are mentioned? You'll hear **gratis** *free* and **opuscolo** *brochure*.

In italiano

Potere *to be able to* is irregular:

singular		plural
posso	1st person	**possiamo**
puoi	2nd person	**potete**
può	3rd person	**possono**

The verb following **potere** is in the infinitive.

Si può...? *Can one...?* is often used instead of **posso** or **possiamo** to ask if you can do something:

Si può parcheggiare qui? *Can I/you/we park here?* **G16**

... and advice

4   1•32 Listen to the key language:

(Che) cosa c'è da fare/vedere?   What is there to do/see?
Se vi piace ...   If you like ...
Se vi interessa ...   If you're interested in ...
Se preferite ...   If you prefer...
Potete ...   You can ...
Da non mancare.   Not to be missed.

5   1•33 As you listen to more tourists making enquiries at the **APT**, listen out for the following and tick them as you hear them.

 in macchina   **in bicicletta**   **sentiero natura**   **vigneto**

riserva marina   **castello medioevale**   **sagra della lumaca**

---

6   1•33 Now read the response and fill the gaps.

● **Cosa c'è da fare nella zona?**
◆ **Beh, se .... passeggiare, c'è il sentiero natura. Se .... esplorare in macchina – o in bicicletta – ci sono tantissime cose da vedere. .... visitare la riserva marina o il castello medioevale, oppure potete .... a un vigneto. A otto chilometri da qui c'è il nuovo centro di parapendio. No? Beh ... da non mancare se la cultura locale ...., sabato c'è la sagra della lumaca a Cavriglia.**

Talking about leisure interests

1   1•34 Listen to the key language:

Cosa ti piace fare?	What do you like doing?
Mi piace soprattutto ...	I particularly like ...
Ti interessano gli sport?	Are you interested in sports?
Le interessa il parapendio?	Are you interested in paragliding?
Vi interessa il calcio?	Are you (pl) interested in football?
Ci interessa/interessano ...	We're interested in ... (sing/pl)

2   1•35 Listen as Nico, Luisa and Isabella talk about what they like to do, and make a note of their interests. Use the words in the box to help you. **Tifoso** is a *fan*.

> **fare kung-fu** *do kung-fu*   **calcio** *football*
> **fare windsurf** *go windsurfing*   **nuotare** *swimming*
> **fare trekking** *go rambling*

In italiano

The way to say *I'm interested in nature* is **mi interessa la natura**, literally *nature interests me*. Replacing **mi** with **ti**, **le**, **ci** or **vi** does not disturb the rest of the sentence:

Le interessa la natura? *Are you interested in nature?*
Ci interessa la natura. *We're interested in nature.*

Piace/piacciono works in the same way: **Mi piace lo sci** *I like skiing*; **Vi piace la vela?** *Do you like sailing?*

G32

3   1•36 Read the following carefully, then listen to Isabella's father talking about the family's interest in trekking in Italy's National Parks, and tick the phrases as you hear them.

- passeggiare lungo i sentieri
- fare trekking
- essere in contatto con la natura
- ammirare il panorama
- godere della pace e del silenzio
- osservare l'orso bruno
- scoprire paesini caratteristici

4   Have a go at talking about your interests – your own and any that you share with other people.

Planning an activity

1 **1•37** Listen to the key language:

Bisogna ...	You need to ...
È consigliabile ...	It's advisable ...
È necessario ...	It's necessary ...
Posso pagare con ...?	Can I pay by ...?
Si può prenotare qui?	Can I book here?
Mi può fare uno sconto?	Can you give me a discount?

2 **1•38** At the **APT**, someone wants to book a guided walk in the nature reserve: **Mi interessa fare un'escursione guidata nella riserva. Si può prenotare qui?** Listen a couple of times to the information she's given, then identify which of the phrases below was not mentioned. Then read the transcript of the conversation on page 111.

- You don't need to book.
- There's a walk every day.
- They start at 9am.
- They last four hours.
- You need to bring food and water.
- It's important to wear suitable shoes.
- It's advisable to bring a sweater or a sweatshirt.

3 **1•39** Matteo is telling Luisa about his plans for exploring the area with a friend tomorrow. Listen and decide what prompts him to say **Caspita!**

M Domani andiamo in giro, per esplorare un po'.
L A piedi o in macchina? Oppure potete noleggiare un motorino.
M Esplorare in motorino! Caspita!

4 **1•40** Matteo's friend wasn't as keen on hiring a **motorino**, so they decide to hire bikes. Listen as Matteo rings the hire company and note:

a how long they want the bikes for;
b how much it costs per bike;
c how much discount he is offered.

> ### NOLEGGIO BICICLETTE
>
> **Costi di noleggio**
> 1 ora   €5,00
> 1 giorno €15,00
>
> **Sconti**
> 15% per gruppi di minimo 5 biciclette
>
> **Documenti necessari**
> Documento in corso di validità
> Carta di credito (Deposito cauzionale €300)

put it **all together**

1   Match the two halves.

a	Mi piacciono	1	indossare scarpe adatte.
b	Si può	2	con la carta di credito?
c	Avete	3	fare uno sconto?
d	Mi interessa	4	prenotare qui?
e	Mi può	5	una piantina della città?
f	È consigliabile	6	gli sport estremi.
g	Possiamo pagare	7	l'Italia.

2   Complete the question: ...... **piace questa foto?** as if you were talking to:

   a   your niece Anna;
   b   Anna and her friend Elena;
   c   your elderly neighbours;
   d   a business acquaintance;
   e   your partner.

3   Your neighbour's granddaughter has just received an email from a new friend in Italy and can't read it. Explain to her what this section says, using the glossary for any new words.

Non ho molti passatempi. Mi piace uscire con gli amici, andare in città, fare shopping. Ci piace soprattutto andare in spiaggia a Borgo Marina dove giochiamo a pallavolo e prendiamo il sole. Si può fare windsurf ma non sono molto brava.

Mi interessa la musica perché mia zia è cantante.
E mi piace la danza – frequento una classe di danza moderna ogni mercoledì. E tu? Cosa ti piace fare?

1 1•41 Imagine you're at the tourist office in L'Aquila in Abruzzo. You're with a friend, so you'll be using *we*.

- **Buongiorno. Posso aiutarvi?**
- ◆ Greet her and ask if they have a food and wine guide.
- **Ecco ... con tutti i ristoranti e le trattorie.**
- ◆ Ask if there's a good restaurant nearby.
- **Se vi piace la cucina italiana tradizionale, la Trattoria Moretta ha una buona reputazione.**
- ◆ Now ask what there is to do in L'Aquila.
- **Ah ... ci sono tante cose da vedere, da fare. Vi do questa guida e un calendario degli eventi.**
- ◆ Say you're interested in nature. Ask if it's possible to go on a guided tour in the National Park.
- **Nel Parco del Gran Sasso ci sono escursioni a piedi, a cavallo o in mountain bike. Ecco i dettagli. È consigliabile prenotare ... e indossare scarpe comode!**
- ◆ You also want transport. Ask if it's possible to hire a scooter.
- **Sì, in via Matteotti ... guardi sulla piantina, qui.**

2 1•42 You're chatting to Alessandro, who you've met on holiday. He's just suggested **Diamoci del tu**.

- ● Ask him what he does at the weekend.
- ◆ **Beh ... un po' di shopping, esco con amici – andiamo al cinema, in discoteca ... mangiamo al ristorante.**
- ● Ask him if he likes sports (**gli sport**).
- ◆ **Sì, mi piace nuotare, giocare a pallavolo. Lo sci nautico anche.**
- ● Ask him if he's interested in football.
- ◆ **Il calcio? Ma senz'altro – sono tifoso della Juventus. Ma dimmi, cosa fai tu nel tempo libero?**

3 Using the glossary, tell an English-speaking friend what Alessandro does at the weekend, then practise replying to his question: **Cosa fai tu nel tempo libero?** *What do you do in your spare time?*

quiz

1 What does **enogastronomia** refer to?

2 Would you use **può** or **puoi** with **lei**?

3 To ask a group of people if they're interested in football, would you use **ti interessano**, **vi interessa** or **vi interessano**?

4 Would you read, wear or eat **una felpa**?

5 What do **avete**, **preferite** and **chiamate** have in common?

6 **Guida**, **elenco**, **opuscolo**, **orario**, **sagra**. Which is the odd one out and why?

7 .... is an alternative to **posso** and **possiamo** to ask if you can do something.

8 What does **Da non mancare** mean?

Now check whether you can ...

- ask for information and advice in a tourist office
- ask about/say what you and other people can do
- arrange an activity
- talk about what you like to do in your spare time
- ask others about their leisure interests
- say *you* (**voi**) do something if you're given the infinitive of a verb

The official website of the Italian Tourist Board, which you can find at **www.enit.it**, is full of fascinating facts and figures about Italy. Click on the Italian flag for information in Italian about leisure activities, nature, history, food or art. Try to skim read, i.e. don't get hung up on single words that you don't understand, but try to get the flow of the passage. If you then click on the British flag you'll find the same information in English and you can compare the two.

Che bella casa!

reading property descriptions

describing a property

enquiring about renting a villa

showing someone round a house

In Italia ...

large numbers of visitors prefer to **prendere in affitto** *rent* than stay in a hotel. And statistics show that they're buying property in increasing numbers too, unable to resist the **villa al mare**, the **rustico** *country pad* in **posizione panoramica**, the **casa rurale con terreno** *house in the country with land* or, for the more intrepid, the **cascina da ristrutturare** *farmhouse in need of renovation*.

What motivates them: **il clima, la cultura, il paesaggio, la cucina, i prezzi, lo stile italiano** or ...?

Reading property descriptions

VENDESI

VILLA VISTA MARE DI NUOVA COSTRUZIONE

Villa indipendente di nuova costruzione su due livelli, con 3 camere, 2 bagni, ampio box auto e giardino. In zona collinare a circa 2km dal mare, in posizione panoramica con vista mare. **Prezzo: €600.000**

OPPORTUNITÀ IRRIPETIBILE. Vendesi appartamento in un bellissimo palazzo antico completamente ristrutturato, nel cuore del centro storico. Ingresso, salone doppio, due camere, bagno + bagno di servizio, cucina-soggiorno, terrazzo. **Prezzo: da negoziare**

VILLETTA A SCHIERA, bilocale, di recente costruzione. Posizione centralissima. **Prezzo: €280.000**

IN ZONA PANORAMICA E COMODA, a 2km dal centro paese, vendiamo rustico perfettamente ristrutturato, con ingresso, soggiorno, sala da pranzo, cucina, 4 camere, 2 bagni, cantina di 50mq, garage e giardino. Posizione soleggiata, tranquilla ma non isolata. **Prezzo: €840.000**

ANTICO MULINO CON TERRENO DA RISTRUTTURARE

Vecchio mulino in pietra, da ristrutturare. Circostante terreno di 4.000mq. Nella massima tranquillità ma non isolato e con comodo accesso in auto. Ideale come agriturismo o Bed & Breakfast. **Prezzo: da negoziare**

1   Look at the property profiles from the **agenzia immobiliare** *estate agent's* and see how many of the words you know or can guess by thinking of English agents' terminology. Then work through the profiles systematically, consulting the glossary where you need to, and list:

   a   five types of house
   b   nine different rooms
   c   three outside features
   d   eight adjectives used to describe location

Describing a property

1 **1•43** Listen to the key language:

Com'è ...?	What's ... like?
(Mi) può descrivere ...	Can you describe (for me) ...
... la sua casa?	... your house? (**lei**)
... la tua/la vostra casa?	... your house? (**tu/voi**)
Si trova ...	It's (located) ...
Hanno ...	They have ...

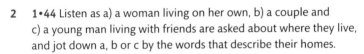

2 **1•44** Listen as a) a woman living on her own, b) a couple and c) a young man living with friends are asked about where they live, and jot down a, b or c by the words that describe their homes.

villa singola	da ristrutturare	comodo
rustico	moderno	tranquillo
palazzo	centrale	panoramico
villetta a schiera	di nuova costruzione	antico
cascina	vecchio	conveniente

Except when talking about one member of the family, the words for *my, your, our,* etc. have the definite article in front of them:

mio figlio but **il mio lavoro**

tua nonna but **la tua macchina**

Mio, tuo, suo, nostro *our* and **vostro** agree with what's owned not with the owner. *My car* is always **la mia macchina**.

Loro *their* never changes: **la loro casa; le loro case** and always has the definite article: **il loro padre** *their father*. **G9**

In italiano

---

3 **1•45** The couple describe their house in more detail. Listen and decide:

- how many bedrooms it has,
- how many bathrooms,
- whether it has a garage,
- what's special about the terrace.

Enquiring about renting a villa

1   Anna Kiel finds an advert for the Villa Adriana, which is **in affitto** to let.

Villa Adriana si trova a quindici minuti dal mare e con comodo accesso a negozi, supermercato, bar e pizzeria. Bella casa spaziosa in stile tradizionale, buon punto di partenza per escursioni alla Riserva Natura. Può ospitare da 6 a 9 persone. Soggiorno minimo 7 giorni.

Piano terra: ampio soggiorno con camino e divano letto doppio, cucina attrezzata (4 fuochi, forno, freezer, lavastoviglie), bagno con doccia attrezzato per disabili.

Primo piano: camera matrimoniale (+ letto singolo), 2 camere doppie (una con letti a castello), bagno.

Ampio spazio esterno, con parcheggio, giardino e terrazzo con vista panoramica.

Prezzi: Gen-Mar €775/Apr-Giu €875/Lug-Ago €1050/Set-Ott €875

How would Anna tell her partner, in English:
a   how many bedrooms and bathrooms the villa has,
b   how far it is from the sea,
c   whether there's anywhere to park the car,
d   what there is to do locally,
e   how much it will cost for a week in August?

2   1•46 Listen to the key language:

Pronto	Hello (on the phone)
Penso di ...	I'm thinking of ...
... prendere in affitto ...	... renting ...
Quanti/Quante ...?	How many ... ? (m/f)
Ce ne sono ... *	There are ... (of them)

* **ne** means of it/of them, often omitted in English.

3   1•47 Anna rings another villa. Listen and answer the questions below.

a   **Quante camere ci sono?**   e   **C'è la lavastoviglie?**
b   **Quanti bagni ci sono?**   f   **È vicino al mare?**
c   **C'è un giardino?**   g   **Quanto costa alla settimana?**
d   **Si può parcheggiare?**

Showing someone round a house

1 **1•48** Listen to the key language:

Che bello!	How lovely!
Che bella stanza!	What a beautiful room!
È molto/un po'...	It's very/a bit ...
È piuttosto/così ...	It's rather/so ...
Accomodatevi.	Make yourselves at home.
Buona permanenza.	Enjoy your stay.

2 **1•49** Anna's family decide to rent the Villa Adriana. Listen as they're shown round, then fit **molto**, **un po'**, **così** and **piuttosto** into the gaps.

- Allora, ecco il soggiorno, con il camino e la finestra con vista panoramica.
- ◆ Che bella stanza! È ...... spaziosa – e che vista!
- Qui abbiamo la cucina, ... spaziosa anche. Tutto è nuovo di quest'anno: il forno, la lavastoviglie, il frigo.
- ◆ Non c'è la lavatrice?
- Ma sì, si trova nel bagno di servizio. L'asciugabiancheria anche. Ecco le camere, questa con i letti gemelli e questa a sinistra con i letti a castello.
- ◆ Questa è ...... piccola.
- È ...... compatta, sì. Qui abbiamo la camera principale. E non dimenticate che il divano nel soggiorno è un divano letto.

> Words like **piuttosto** and **così** are adverbs, not adjectives, so their endings don't change. Look out though for **molto**, which can be either. As an adverb it means *very*, but as an adjective it means *a lot of* or *many* and agrees with what it describes: **molta acqua**, **molti ristoranti**.
>
> **G11**

In italiano

3 **1•50** Listening out for the key words **cento** *hundred/hundreds* and **mila** *thousands*, write down how much these properties cost.

a	villetta bifamiliare *semi-detached* con garage	....
b	splendido appartamento di nuova costruzione	....
c	rustico perfettamente ristrutturato	....
d	villa, 5 locali	....
e	casa colonica in posizione panoramica	....

put it all together

1   From this list of words, find seven pairs of opposites, e.g.
    grande and **piccolo**. You're left with one word – what is it and
    what does it mean in English?

cantina	centrale	compatto	asciugabiancheria
grande	isolato	lavatrice	mare
nuovo	piccolo	rurale	spazioso
urbano	vecchio	montagna	

2   What's the Italian for the areas labelled a–h?

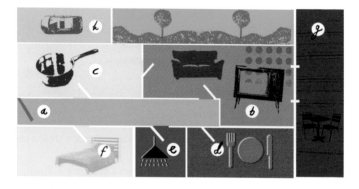

3   Write in Italian a profile of these two properties, of the kind
    used to advertise places **vendesi** *for sale* or **affitasi** *to let*.

> **FOR SALE** Villa, new-build, with sea view, 5 mins from
> the sea. Garden + sunny terrace. 3 beds, 2 baths.

> **TO LET** Spacious country house in scenic location,
> peaceful but not isolated. Ground floor: entrance, sitting
> room, fitted kitchen, cloakroom/utility room. 1st floor:
> 4 bedrooms, bathroom. Large garden + garage.

4   Now write a similar short description of your home.

now you're talking!

1   1•51 You call the Villa Marina for information.

- **Villa Marina. Pronto.**
- ◆ Say you're thinking of renting a house in Italy. Ask if he'll describe the Villa Marina for you.
- **È una bellissima villetta con giardino e terrazzo.**
- ◆ Ask if it's near the sea.
- **Si trova a tre o quattro chilometri da una splendida spiaggia.**
- ◆ Ask how much it costs per week.
- **€1300.**
- ◆ It's not cheap. Ask how many bedrooms there are.
- **Ce ne sono tre. Comunque, può ospitare fino a nove persone.**
- ◆ And how many bathrooms?
- **C'è il bagno principale al primo piano.**
- ◆ Ask if there's a washing machine.
- **Ma certo.**
- ◆ You don't want to be washing up on your holiday. Is there a dishwasher?
- **No, non c'è.**
- ◆ You've heard enough! Say 'Well, thank you and goodbye'.

2   1•52 You end up staying in a house in the country near Stresa. Someone you meet asks what it's like.

- **Com'è la sua casa?**
- ◆ Say it's a country place.
- **Dove si trova?**
- ◆ Say it's ten kilometres from Stresa.
- **È grande la casa? Quante camere ci sono?**
- ◆ Say there are six.
- **Sei! E quanti bagni?**
- ◆ Say there are five.
- **Bello! Avete un giardino?**
- ◆ Say there's a small garden and a terrace.
- **Allora – arrivederci e buona permanenza.**

quiz

1   What sort of building is a **palazzo**?

2   If a property is **da ristrutturare**, what state is it in?

3   What's another Italian word for **un box**?

4   Do you wash clothes in a **lavatrice** or a **lavastoviglie**?

5   When talking to a couple about their **villa**, do you use **la tua**, **la sua** or **la vostra**?

6   How would you say to them *What a beautiful house!*?

7   To say *It's rather expensive* what word do you need in the gap?
    È .... **caro**.

8   Which is the odd one out: **collinare**, **comodo**, **conveniente**?

Now check whether you can ...

- understand the key words in property descriptions
- make enquiries about renting a villa
- describe your own home
- show someone round your house
- comment on a house and pay a compliment to its owner
- understand prices in hundreds and thousands of euros

Memory-training techniques can be used to good effect when learning a language. Start with a simple sentence such as **Vorrei una casa in Italia** then add to it in small increments: **Vorrei una casa in Italia con un terrazzo**, adding more as you mentally zoom in: **Vorrei una casa in Italia con un terrazzo e una cucina grande ... e tre bagni ... e una cantina** – until you're describing your ideal property in detail and creating a substantial sentence in Italian.

In più 2

1   Italy's 20 **regioni** each have a distinct character. Read about three of them, see if you can work out which they are and match them to the numbers on the map. (They're all in *In più 1*.)

a   La .... è un'isola del Mar Mediterraneo, abitata da circa 5 milioni di persone. In questa regione si trovano ricchezze archeologiche e magnifiche antichità greche, per esempio il Tempio della Concordia ad Agrigento. Il capoluogo è Palermo.

b   Questa regione è divisa in quattro province: L'Aquila, Pescara, Chieti e Teramo. È conosciuta per i quattro grandi parchi nazionali, per gli sport invernali nelle montagne e per il vino rosso Montepulciano d'............ Confina a nord con le Marche e ad est con il mare Adriatico.

c   Questa regione si trova nell'Italia centrale, confina a nord-ovest con la Liguria, a nord con l'Emilia-Romagna, a est con le Marche e l'Umbria, a sud con il Lazio. Il capoluogo della .... è famoso per ricchezze storiche, artistiche e culturali come il magnifico Duomo, gli Uffizi, il Ponte Vecchio. In inglese si chiama spesso Chiantishire.

- Adjectives ending in **-co** after a consonant, such as **ricco** *rich*, add h in the plural, keeping the same sound: **ricchi, ricche**.
- Adjectives ending in **-co** after a vowel, such as **storico** *historic*, **greco** *Greek*, add h in the feminine plural: **le città storiche** but **i centri storici**.

Most nouns ending in **-ca, -co, -ga** and **-go** also add h in the plural: **il fuoco** *fire, burner* ▸ **i fuochi**; **il luogo** *place* ▸ **i luoghi**.

In italiano

2   Keith and Bella Lee are planning a self-catering walking holiday in Abruzzo with two friends. They've agreed what they want and are looking for the right house. Read the information on these two and put a ✓ or ✗ against them to show whether they meet the criteria. If no information is available, put a ?.

	1	2
a within reach of Gran Sasso National Park		
b property with character		
c quiet location		
d shops not too far		
e somewhere to eat outside		
f car parking		
g sleeps four comfortably		
h two bathrooms		
i fully equipped kitchen		
j heating (it can be cold in the mountains)		

1

IN AFFITTO casa indipendente di nuova costruzione in piccolo paese montano, immerso nella natura del Parco Gran Sasso.
Completamente arredato con 4-5 posti letto, l'alloggio comprende piccolo ingresso, soggiorno, ampia cucina rustica (4 fuochi, forno, freezer, lavastoviglie), bagno + bagno di servizio, 2 camere da letto (con armadi a muro). Vista delle montagne dal piccolo terrazzo. Box auto a richiesta. Rif. No. AL 54

2

IN AFFITTO La Torre Vecchia, completamente restaurata. Dista 12km dal Gran Sasso, dove ci sono delle piste da sci e da snowboard veramente belle.
Con splendido panorama sulla vallata, La Torre è arredata con cura e raffinatezza. L'alloggio è composto da ampio soggiorno con grande camino e angolo cottura, 6 posti letto, 2 bagni.
Centro commerciale con supermercato + centro sportivo con piscina a 2 km; fermata bus a 200m. Possibilità di garage. Rif. 780.

3 The Lees like the look of **La Torre Vecchia** and write to the **proprietario** *owner*, asking for more information. See if you can read the letter without using the glossary, then check the English translation on page 114. **Vorremmo** is the **noi** form of **vorrei**.

---

18 giugno 2007

Signor Ignazio Vissani
La Torre Vecchia
Abruzzo

Gentile Signor Vissani,

Mi interessa trascorrere due settimane presso La Torre Vecchia con mia moglie e due amici. Mi può dire se è disponibile dal 22 settembre al 6 ottobre? Può confermare la quota settimanale per questo periodo, incluso l'uso di un garage?

Vorremmo anche sapere se c'è una lavatrice e se l'angolo cottura dispone di un freezer.

Distinti saluti,

Keith Lee

---

4 Using this letter as your model, write a letter to signor Vissani, saying:

- you and three friends would like to spend a week at the Torre Vecchia between July 28th and 4th August;
- you want to know the price, including **l'assicurazione** (f) insurance
- you'd like to know how many bedrooms there are and if there's a dishwasher.

5 Signor Vissani's reply, confirming availability, included this information about the kitchen facilities. Read it, check any new words in the glossary, then close the book and have a go at saying what's in your own kitchen, starting **La mia cucina ....**

L'angolo cottura dispone di cucina elettrica con quattro fuochi e forno, freezer, frigorifero, microonde, lavastoviglie, macchina per il caffè e stoviglie.

There's no difference between *his*, *her* and *your* (**lei**) when you're talking about possession:

il suo nome	*his/her/your name*
la sua macchina	*his/her/your car*
i suoi passatempi	*his/her/your hobbies*
le sue idee	*his/her/your ideas*

Any potential confusion can be avoided by saying **la macchina di Franco**, **i passatempi di Anna**, **le idee di lei**.

G9

6 With his reply, Signor Vissani sent a checklist of essentials for the Lees' trekking holiday.

In the left column, choose **il mio**, **la mia**, **i miei** or **le mie** as if Keith or Bella were saying which items he or she should pack.
In the middle column, choose **il suo**, **la sua**, **i suoi** or **le sue** as if you were saying which items either of them should pack.

my	his/her		
			zaino
			torcia
			scarpe da trekking
			cappello
			guanti
			giacca impermeabile
			occhiali da sole

7 The compass **bussola** (f sing) and binoculars **binocolo** (m sing) belong to both of them. Do they need **il nostro**, **la nostra**, **i nostri** or **le nostre** to say *our compass* and *our binoculars*?

Secondo me ...

shopping for clothes

... and shoes and bags

expressing your opinion

... and making comparisons

In Italia ...

given its national dedication to **lo stile** and the influence of its world-famous **stilisti** *fashion designers*, it's hardly surprising that shopping for clothes and accessories can be a pleasurable experience.

A lot of English words in everyday use have settled into Italian patterns: **un top** is masculine, whereas **una polo** is short for **una camicia polo** *polo shirt* and therefore feminine. **Un (paio di) jeans** is *a pair of jeans* but the word **jeans** is used for denim in general and even as a colour.

Shopping for clothes

1 1•53 Listen to the key language:

Cerco .../Desidero ...	I'm looking for .../I want ...
un pantalone	some trousers
una camicia/giacca bianca	a white shirt/jacket
un top/una maglia di lana	a top/jumper in wool
taglia quaranta	size 40
Sto guardando.	I'm just browsing.

2 1•54 Get familiar with the words below, listen to some conversations heard in clothes shops and note in English what people are buying.

bianco *white*	**nero** *black*	**grigio** *grey*	**verde** *green*
rosso *red*	**giallo** *yellow*	**azzurro** *blue*	**blu** *navy*

lino *linen*	**pura lana** *pure wool*	**puro cotone** *pure cotton*
seta *silk*	**cachemire** *cashmere*	

	articolo	colore	tessuto *fabric*	taglia *size*
a				
b				
c				
d				
e				
f				

In italiano

The endings of some colour adjectives never change:

- foreign words, e.g. **blu**: **le scarpe blu**;
- nouns used as colours, e.g. the flowers **rosa** and **viola**
- a colour + another adjective, e.g. **verde scuro** *dark green*, **giallo canarino** *canary yellow*: **una camicia giallo canarino**. **G5**

3 1•55 Listen to a couple out shopping then answer these questions:

a What are they looking for?
b What two colours do they ask for?
c Who is it for?
d How much does it cost?

... and shoes and bags

4 **1•56** Listen to the key language:

Vorrei provare ...	I'd like to try ... on.
Che numero porta?	What size (shoes) do you take?
Vorrebbe provarli?	Would you like to try them on?
Voglio cambiarlo.	I want to change it.
Posso vederlo/a?	Can I see it?

5 **1•57** In a shoe shop a customer sees some **stivali** *boots* she likes and wants to try them on. Listen and jot down what size she takes, the sizes of the boots they have in stock and what different colour she's offered.

> *It* **lo** (m) or **la** (f) and *them* **li** (m) and **le** (f) are normally found in front of the verb:
>
> **Il cachemire? Lo** lavo a mano. *Cashmere? I wash it by hand.*
> **Le mie scarpe? Le** compro a Milano. *My shoes? I buy them in Milan.*
>
> But when the verb's in the infinitive, they can go at the end:
>
> **Vorrebbe provarla?** *Would you like to try it on?* (la camicia)
> **Vorrebbe provarli?** *Would you like to try them on?* (gli stivali) **G33**

In italiano

6 Using the glossary, read this advert for **uno zaino** *a backpack*.

a Underline the adjectives used to describe the backpack.

b What's the Italian for zip, pocket and pockets?

> **Zaino sport** leggero di tessuto impermeabile. Lavabile. Comodo e capiente; tasca centrale frontale con cerniera rinforzata; 2 tasche laterali; 2 tasche interne (una con chiusura a cerniera); tasca per telefono cellulare.

7 **1•58** A customer saying **Ho comprato questo zaino** *I bought this backpack* has brought it back to the shop because something is **rotto** *broken*. Listen and note in English what's wrong. Listen again and note in Italian the words he uses to say he wants to change it.

Expressing your opinion

1 1•59 Listen to the key language:

Cosa pensi di questo?	What do you think of this?
Mi va bene questo?	Does this one fit me?
Secondo me ...	In my opinion ...
È abbastanza lungo/corto.	It's long/short enough.
È troppo vivace/spento.	It's too bright/pale.
Quello lì ti va/sta meglio.	That one fits/suits you better.

2 1•60 Dino Senesi is shopping for an outfit for his wedding, with his mother Grazia and his sister Susanna. Listen and tick the items of clothing you hear. Listen out too for Susanna saying **a me piace** I like.

 camicia   cravatta   gilet   giacca

pantalone   scarpe   cravatta a farfalla

One in phrases like *this one* or *the black ones* is not translated.

Secondo me, questo ti va bene. *In my view, this one fits you.*
Preferisco quello. *I prefer that one.*
Scarpe? Mi piacciono le nere. *Shoes? I like the black ones.*

When things are being compared, **lì** *there* can be added to **quello**, and **qui** *here* to **questo: Questa qui o quella lì?**   **G10**

3 1•60 Listen again and insert the right form of **questo** or **quello**.

D Mamma, cosa pensi di .... giacca? Mi va bene?
G Secondo me, è un po' grande. Le maniche sono troppo lunghe.
S Non mi piace. Secondo me, ... qui ti sta meglio.
D Susanna, non fare la cretina. .... lì è troppo vivace. Mamma,
.... pantalone – è abbastanza lungo? Non è troppo corto?
G No, è perfetto con .... scarpe nere. Cosa pensi di ....
cravatta?
D Boh. Un po' spenta.
S A me piace .... cravatta a farfalla. Con una bella camicia
bianca e un gilet giallo canarino.

... and making comparisons

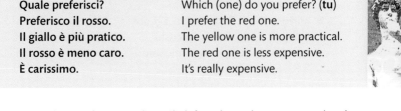

4 1•61 Listen to the key language:

Quale vestito preferisce?	Which dress do you prefer? (**lei**)
Quale preferisci?	Which (one) do you prefer? (**tu**)
Preferisco il rosso.	I prefer the red one.
Il giallo è più pratico.	The yellow one is more practical.
Il rosso è meno caro.	The red one is less expensive.
È carissimo.	It's really expensive.

5 1•62 It's Grazia's turn to shop. She's found two dresses, one red and one yellow, and she and Susanna are discussing them while the **commesso** *shop assistant* hovers. Listen, then summarise in English what Grazia thinks of each dress.

C Quale vestito preferisce, signora?

G Il rosso è più pratico.

S Io preferisco il giallo. È più sexy, più stravagante.

G Il giallo è un po' stretto, il rosso è più comodo.

S Mamma, secondo me, il rosso è un po' corto per te.

G È vero, il giallo è più lungo. Ma è carissimo questo giallo – però meno caro del rosso. Mah!

To compare things, you use **più** *more* with the adjective:
più elegante *more stylish*, **più stretto** *tighter*.

Than is **di** or, when followed by *the*, **del**, **della**, etc.
La giacca è più cara del vestito. *The jacket is more expensive than the dress.*

Meno *less* is also used: **È meno pratico.** *It's less practical.*
Il/la più/meno means *the most/the least*:
La più elegante *the most stylish*, **il meno pratico** *the least practical.*

G12

In italiano

---

6 1•63 Grazia tries on one more dress, which Susanna and the shop assistant feel very differently about. Listen and try to pick out the adjectives used by both of them to describe it. If you need help, the transcript's on page 116.

put it all together

1 What's the opposite of these (in Italian)?

a meno   e nero

b corto   f stravagante

c spento   g piccolo

d esterno   h antiquato

2 Put the right ending on the adjectives.

a Mi sta bene quest...... giacca bianc......?

b Quell...... cravatta è più spent.......

c Ti piacciono le scarpe ner......?

d Preferisci il top verd...... o il ross......?

e Gli stivali sono un po' grand.......

f Posso provare la maglia con le maniche lung......?

g Secondo me, lo zaino blu è meno capient.......

h Che pensi del vestito giall......?

3 Rewrite these sentences, replacing the shaded words with *it* or *them* and making changes as necessary to the word order. **Pagare** means *to pay* or *to pay for*, depending on the context.

a Compro i miei vestiti a Milano.

b Lavo questa maglia a mano.

c Posso cambiare questo jeans?

d Voglio pagare gli stivali neri.

e Paga questa giacca con carta di credito?

f Vorrei provare le scarpe blu.

4 How would you say you're looking for:

- jeans in size 38;
- a white linen shirt;
- a navy pure wool jacket, size 40;
- a lightweight waterproof rucksack with internal pockets?

now you're talking!

1 **1•64** You're out shopping for clothes.

- **Posso aiutarla?**
- ◆ Say you're looking for a jacket.
- **Che taglia?**
- ◆ You're a 46.
- **Allora. Abbiamo giacche di cotone, lino, viscosa, poliestere, jeans ... o forse desidera una giacca di lana?**
- ◆ Say yes, you'd like a wool jacket.
- **E che colore?**
- ◆ You're not entirely sure. Say black or navy.
- **Abbiamo questa blu di pura lana vergine, o questa qui di lana con 40% cachemire.**
- ◆ Ask if you can try the black one on.
- **Si accomodi – è bellissima questa qui.**
- ◆ Ask how much it costs.
- **Oh, il prezzo è molto ragionevole, trecentonovanta euro.**

2 **1•65** On to another shop to change a wallet (**un portafogli**).

- **C'è un problema?**
- ◆ Say yes, this is broken and you'd like to change it.
- **Posso vederlo?**
- ◆ Point to the broken fastening and say 'here'.
- **Sfortunatamente non ne abbiamo altri di questo tipo. Le piace questo qui?**
- ◆ Ask your friend what she thinks of this one.
- **Secondo me è un po' piccolo.**

3 **1•66** To a third shop where your friend tries on a pair of boots.

- **Ti piacciono questi? Mi stanno bene?**
- ◆ She's asking whether they suit her. Say that in your opinion they're a bit tight.
- **Ma sono così belli. E c'è uno sconto del 25%.**
- ◆ You find a different pair and tell her you prefer these ... and they're less expensive.
- **Caspita! Sono fantastici.**

quiz

1 In a shop, how would you say you're just browsing?

2 What word do you use to say you're looking for something? What's the infinitive? And how would you spell the **noi** form?

3 If you're being asked for your size, where would you expect to hear a) **Che taglia?** and b) **Che numero?**

4 What colour do you think **verde smeraldo** is?

5 Referring to a jacket, how would you say you don't like the grey one?

6 **La camicia è più cara ...... giacca.** What's the missing word?

7 What's the subtle difference between **mi piace** and **a me piace**?

8 What's the Italian for a zip?

Now check whether you can ...

- say you're looking for something in a shop or just browsing
- use adjectives to describe
- express your opinion and ask for someone else's
- compare things using **più** and **meno**
- differentiate between *this one* and *that one*
- use *it* and *them* in the correct position
- express a preference

Being able to give an opinion in a new language is a great step forward. Get used to saying in Italian what you think: comment on the news using **secondo me** and adjectives such as **splendido**, **tragico**, **ridicolo** or **meraviglioso**.

Try commenting on the contents of your wardrobe: describing clothes as **nuovo** *new*, **vecchio** *old* or even **antiquato**, comparing them using **più** and **meno**, and perhaps evaluating them as **ideale** or **perfetto** or **un disastro**!

Ho smarrito il portatile

asking the way

... and following directions

explaining what's happened

reporting a problem

In Italia ...

if you lose your **portatile** *laptop*, **portafogli** *wallet/purse* or **telefonino** *mobile phone*, you'll need to **fare una denuncia** *report the incident*. Unless it constitutes an emergency – in which case you ring 113 – your first port of call will be the nearest **questura** *police station*. This is the headquarters of the **Polizia di Stato** *national police*, who operate as a separate force from the **Carabinieri** *military police*, who deal with general crime and public order. Separate again are the **Vigili Urbani**, who direct traffic and parking in towns, while the **Polizia Stradale** patrol the motorways.

Asking the way

1   2•1 Listen to the key language:

Mi/Ci può aiutare?	Can you help me/us?
Dove si trova ...?	Where's ... (located)?
Vediamo ...	Let's see ...
Dobbiamo ...	We have to ...
Dovete ...	You have to ... (**voi**)
Avete capito?	Have you understood? (**voi**)

2   2•2 Leo and his wife Stella are looking for the **questura** to report a lost **portatile**. The rambling directions they're given by a passer-by include some of the following phrases. After you've thoroughly familiarised yourself with these, listen and tick them off as you hear them.

sulla vostra sinistra *on your left*	**girate** *you turn*
fino al semaforo *as far as the lights*	**dovete girare** *you have to turn*
in direzione della stazione *towards the station*	**seguite** *you follow*
giù di qui *down here*	**continuate** *you carry on*
lì in fondo *there at the end*	**dovete prendere** *you have to take*
a due passi *very close*	**attraversate** *you cross*

Dovere *to have to/must* is a key irregular verb. Look out for **dobbiamo** *we have to* which is rather different from the rest.

singular		plural	
devo	1st person	dobbiamo	
devi	2nd person	dovete	
deve	3rd person	devono	**G16**

3   2•3 In reply to **Avete capito?** Leo had a go at recapping the directions they were given from notes he'd made. Listen and compare his summary to the original directions. What difference can you find?

... and following directions

4 **2•4** Leo needs to **prelevare contante** *withdraw some cash* on the way, and asks a passer-by for the nearest cashpoint. Listen to what he's told and find it on this map.

5 **2•5** Listen to the key language:

È questa la strada per ...?	Is this the way to ...?
Avete sbagliato strada.	You've gone the wrong way.
Dovete scendere ...	You have to get off (the bus/train) ...

6 **2•6** Stella decides to ask someone else if they're going the right way to the **questura**. Listen, then see if you could interpret the reply for them to make sure they get there.

a The police station is ....
b They can catch the number ...... bus.
c The bus stop is ....
d They need to get off at ....
e The road they need is ....
f The police station is located ....

Explaining what's happened

1   2•7 Listen to the key language:

Ho smarrito/perso ...	I've lost ...
Ho detto ...	I said ...
Cosa hai detto?	What did you say?
Cosa hai fatto?	What have you done?
Hai fatto una denuncia?	Have you reported it?
Roberto ha telefonato.	Roberto (has) phoned.
Vai. Mi raccomando!	Go. For goodness sake!

2   2•8 On the bus Leo rings their friend Stefania to explain why they are going to be late for their five o'clock meeting. Listen to their conversation then fit these verbs in their right places. One is used twice.

ho perso	hai detto	ha telefonato
ho detto	hai fatto	

- Pronto Stefania. Sono Leo.
- ◆ Ciao Leo, ci vediamo alle cinque, vero?
- Senti, Stefania, ... il mio portatile.
- ◆ Come? Cos' .... Cos' ....
- ....: ho smarrito il mio portatile.
- ◆ .... una denuncia? Dovete andare alla questura. Subito.
- Sì, chiaro, sì. Oh – Stefania, Roberto .... ieri.
- ◆ Leo – vai! Mi raccomando! Arrivederci.

In italiano

To talk about the past: i.e. *I (have) lost, Have you seen? Did you see?*, use the present tense of **avere** + the past participle (pp) of the main verb, formed by changing -are ▸ -ato, -ere ▸ -uto and -ire ▸ -ito: aiutare ▸ aiutato; vendere ▸ venduto; capire ▸ capito.

Ho aiutato *I helped*   **Abbiamo capito** *We've understood*
Hai telefonato? *Did you phone?/Have you phoned?*

Some past participles are irregular: **fare ▸ fatto; dire ▸ detto; perdere ▸ perso.**

G21

3   2•9 Leo also rings Franco to say they're running **in ritardo** *late/behind time*. Can you work out why Stella's irritated?

Reporting a problem

1 2•10 Listen to the key language:

(Che) cosa è successo?	What happened?
Eravamo ...	We were ...
Ho messo ...	I put ...
Ha visto ...	Did you see ...
... qualcosa/qualcuno?	... anything/anyone?
Non ho visto niente/nessuno.	I didn't see anything/anyone.
Non c'era.	It wasn't there.

2 At the **questura**, after taking Leo's details, the **agente di polizia** *police officer* takes a statement of what happened. Before you listen, work out the infinitives of these past participles and check their meaning in the glossary: **cercato, compilato, lasciato, appoggiato**. **Visto** and **messo** are irregular; from **vedere** *to see* and **mettere** *to put*.

3 2•11 Listen to Leo's statement then arrange these events in the order they happened, starting with **Eravamo all'ufficio postale.**

 a **ho pagato**
 b **ho compilato il modulo**
 c **ho cercato il portatile**
 d **ho appoggiato il portatile per terra**
 e **ho messo il portafogli e gli occhiali in tasca**

4 Imagine you were at the post office and describe what Leo did, starting **Ha appoggiato ....**

> In **l'ho visto** and **l'ho lasciato**, **l'** is a shortened form of **lo** *it*, referring to **il portatile** (m).
> *It* referring to something feminine is **la** (or **l'**), and the past participle also ends in -a.
> *I've left it* (**la mia borsetta**) is **l'ho lasciata**.   **G34**

In italiano

---

5 What do the following mean?

 a **L'abbiamo lasciato a casa.**   b **L'hanno visto?**

put it all together

1 Which one would you use:

Cosa è successo?

Cosa avete fatto?

Cos'hai detto?

Non ho capito.

Non ho visto niente.

Non ho visto nessuno.

a to ask somebody what he/she said?
b to say you've seen nobody?
c to say you've seen nothing?
d to ask what's happened?
e to say you haven't understood?
f to ask a group of people what they've done?

2 Using the verbs below, how would you say these in Italian?

appoggiare   compilare   finire   capire   lasciare
smarrire   prenotare   seguire   vedere (x 2)

a I've lost my passport.
b Have you seen my shoe? (**tu**)
c We've understood the document.
d Stella has booked the guided tour.
e Have you left the mobile at home? (**tu**)
f Leo put his laptop on the floor.
g I followed the road.
h Have you finished the course? (**lei**)
i They've filled the form in.
j Have you seen the villa? (**voi**)

3 Check your answers, then replace the object of each sentence (i.e. passport) with *it*, e.g. **Ho smarrito il passaporto. L'ho smarrito.** Think about the final letter of the past participle.

now you're **talking!**

1 2•12 You're staying in Italy, and you and your partner need to get to the nearest police station.

- Stop a man in the street and ask if he can help you (both).
- **Mi dica.**
- Find out where the police station's located.
- **In viale Torricelli.**
- You set off, thinking you know where Viale Torricelli is, but now you're lost. Stop a woman and ask if you're on the right road for the police station.
- **Sì, non è lontano. Giù di qui fino al semaforo. Lì dovete girare a sinistra. Seguite la strada fino a via della Vittoria, girate a destra e viale Torricelli si trova sulla vostra sinistra.**
- Tell her you've understood and thank her.

2 Translate the directions to Viale Torricelli for your partner.

3 2•13 Paolo Fulvio, an Italian colleague, leaves you a message saying there's an urgent problem, so you ring him. You know him well so you use **tu**.

- **Pronto. Paolo Fulvio.**
- Ask him what's happened.
- **Stefano ha ...**
- You didn't catch that; ask what he said.
- **Stefano ha smarrito il suo palmare. L'hai visto tu?**
- Say you saw it yesterday. At the restaurant.
- **Ha perso tutto – dati, appuntamenti, numeri di telefono. È molto stressato.**
- Ask if he's left it at Franca's house (**da Franca**).
- **Può darsi, può darsi.** *Could be.* **E voi due, cos'avete fatto oggi?**
- Say you booked a trip to Venice.
- **E dove avete mangiato?**
- Say that at midday you ate at a **trattoria** in Piazza Dante.
- **Mmm ... bello!**

quiz

1 What's the emergency phone number in Italy and what's the Italian for police station?

2 How far is **a due passi**?

3 If somebody says to you **Avete capito?**, what do they want to know?

4 Does **qualcuno** or **qualcosa** mean *something*?

5 If **sbagliare strada** means *to go the wrong way*, what do you think **sbagliare numero** means?

6 How would you ask if you're on the right road to the station?

7 On a bus, to ask where you have to get off is **Dove devo** ....?

8 If **comprare** is *to buy* and **vendere** is *to sell*, how do you say *I bought* and *I sold*?

Now check whether you can ...

- ask the way to a particular place
- follow directions to get there
- say if you've understood or not
- talk about having to do something
- say what you've done
- explain what others have done

You're more than halfway through *Talk Italian 2* – a good time to bring together some of the vocabulary from the six units you've covered. For example:

- say what time you ate **ieri** *yesterday* using the past tense of **fare la colazione** *to have breakfast*, **pranzare** *to have lunch*, **cenare** *to have dinner/supper* or simply using **mangiare**;
- starting with **Oggi ho visto**, list as many things you've seen today as you can, or as many members of your family. (If you haven't seen any of them, say you've seen nobody today.)

In più 3

1   Read the statement Giacomo D'Angelo made after losing his wallet, then find the ten mistakes that somehow made their way into the official **denuncia di smarrimento** lost property report.

> Mi chiamo Giacomo D'Angelo. Abito a Montina, in via Amalfi, 23. Ho trentadue anni; sono nato a Venezia nel 1975. Ieri pomeriggio, lunedì 5 marzo, nel centro sportivo in via Ancona, ho mostrato a Gianni, il mio amico, una bella foto della mia fidanzata Gemma, poi ho messo il mio portafogli (con la foto, 200 euro e la patente di guida dentro) nella tasca della giacca. È di pelle nera questo portafogli ed è nuovissimo; l'ho comprato sabato scorso — ho pagato trentacinque euro. Allora, Gemma mi ha telefonato e ho lasciato la giacca nell'atrio per un attimo, due o tre minuti al massimo. Ho deciso di partire subito … e non ho controllato le mie tasche prima di partire. Non ho visto niente.

---

controllare to check   **decidere** to decide, **deciso** decided
mostrare to show   **trovare** to find

Il sottoscritto | Giacomo D'Ancona

nato a | Verona VE | il | 4 novembre 1975

residente in | piazza Amalfi, 26, Montina | telefono | XXXX 678400

documento di identità | carta d'identità

dichiara ☑ di aver smarrito

il giorno | martedì, 6 marzo | alle ore | 10.00 | in | centro commerciale

dei seguenti oggetti:

portafogli di pelle marrone; contenuti = €300, passaporto, una fotografia. Valore totale €350

modalità:

portafogli lasciato in tasca nell'atrio del centro commerciale

Li (m) and le (f) – *them* – are never shortened to l' and they follow the same rules as *it* – lo, la, l':

- normally in front of the verb, but at the end of an infinitive,
- the ending of the past participle agrees with them.

For example, referring to **le scarpe**:

Le compro a Milano. *I buy them in Milan.*
Vorrei comprar**le**. *I'd like to buy them.*
Le ho comprat**e** ieri. *I bought them yesterday.*

G34

2 Grazia Senesi sent her friend **una mail** *e-mail* to update her on the search for wedding outfits. Even though it contains several new words, first read it straight through to see if you can get an overall impression, then use the glossary to help you with the questions.

-----**Messaggio originale**-----
Da: Grazia Senesi   **Inviato:** giovedì 3 maggio, 17:16
A: Maura Becchi   **Oggetto:** lo shopping

Carissima Maura
Che giornata – sono stanca morta!
Nel negozio Dino e Susanna hanno litigato come un paio di cuccioli. Quando Dino ha provato una bella giacca nera, Susanna l'ha paragonato a un pinguino imperatore! Comunque l'abbiamo comprata (anche un pantalone, una camicia e un bel gilet verde scuro).

Dopo, Susanna ed io abbiamo cercato qualcosa per me, ma non abbiamo comprato niente. Ho trovato un vestito molto elegante in grigio ma non l'ho provato perché Susanna l'ha definito "orrendo e preistorico".
E ho visto un paio di scarpe BELLISSIME – beige, di una pelle morbidissima – ma non le ho comprate (un po' grandi e piuttosto care!!)

Un abbraccio
Grazia

p.s. Giorgio ha comprato un giaccone da sci fantastico.

Vero o falso?

		vero	falso
a	Dino e Susanna hanno comprato due cuccioli.	☐	☐
b	Susanna ha visto un pinguino.	☐	☐
c	Dino ha provato una giacca nera e l'ha comprata.	☐	☐
d	Hanno comprato anche un gilet rosso per Dino.	☐	☐
e	Grazia non ha comprato niente.	☐	☐
f	Susanna ha definito le scarpe preistoriche.	☐	☐
g	Le scarpe costano molto.	☐	☐

3 List in Italian all the examples of *it* and *them* in Grazia's letter.

4 Now write an e-mail to a friend, saying that:

- yesterday you saw a black wool jacket which you tried on;
- you found it a bit big but you bought it,
- however, today you'd like to change it!
- you also bought a white shirt and a pair of black leather shoes,
- but you left them* in the shop!

* when you're talking about a mixture of m and f items (or people) you use the mpl version of adjectives and words like *them*.

In italiano

Bello *beautiful* and **quello** *that* before a noun have endings similar to the definite article:

il	bel	quel
lo	bello	quello
l'	bell'	quell'
la	bella	quella
i	bei	quei
gli	begli	quegli
le	belle	quelle

If **bello** comes after a noun, it's regular: **bello, bella, belli, belle.** **G8**

---

5 Which ending of **bello** and **quello** do you need before these words?

- bello: giacca, appartamento, parco, stivali, cucina
- quello: scarpe, zaino, regione, giardino, vestiti

6 Vuoi un affare? Tutti questi articoli sono di vera pelle o pelle scamosciata *suede*. Ma che cosa sono?

giacca	borsetta	borsone da viaggio
scarpe da sport	marsupio	guanti

a *Da non mancare!! Utile …… di pelle nera, per circonferenza vita 80-120cm. Tasca stretta per banconote + una più ampia per monete e piccoli oggetti. Usato, con la chiusura rotta.*

b Prezzo ridicolo! Bei …… neri da uomo con chiusura in velcro sul polso. Vera pelle (palma) e tessuto (dorso). Taglia XL

c …… di pelle scamosciata beige con cappuccio e imbottitura di pelliccia anche nelle maniche. Usata solo una settimana, praticamente come nuova. Taglia M

d Fantastiche …… numero 45. ULTIMISSIMA VERSIONE di pelle blu con logo argento. Di grande effetto sotto un jeans! Di qualità superiore e quasi nuove. Al negozio costano più di 140€.

e *Tutto di vera pelle fatta a mano …… da donna. Può essere usata a mano o a spalla. 14cm di lunghezza, 10cm di larghezza e 6cm di profondità.*

f Uno splendido …… con rotelle di pelle color champagne. L'interno completamente foderato di pelle scamosciata. Lunghezza 55cm, altezza 35cm. Lo trovate nei negozi a €300!!!

In italiano

Adding an ending to a word is used to great effect in Italian: e.g. -issimo added to an adjective is the equivalent of saying *extremely* in English: bello ▸ bellissimo, cara ▸ carissima.

Endings referring to size are often added to nouns instead of using adjectives. This sometimes changes the gender of the basic word.

- *small*: -ino or -etto: una cucina ▸ un cucinino *a tiny kitchen*, uno zaino ▸ uno zainetto *small backpack*, una borsa *bag* ▸ una borsetta *small handbag*.
- *big*: -one: una giacca ▸ un giaccone *a heavy jacket*, una borsa ▸ un borsone *a holdall*.

Sei mai stato a Capri?

talking about holiday plans

... and the weather

talking about previous holidays

... and describing what happened

In Italia ...

consistent good weather and proximity to **il mare**, **la campagna** and **le montagne** lead to many Italians spending their **vacanze** in Italy. People who live **in città** pack their bags in August and head **al mare** or **in montagna**. A winter favourite is **la settimana bianca** *winter sports holiday*; literally *white week*.

If you're planning an outdoor activity you'll need to understand **le previsioni meteo** *weather forecast*, whether you're interested in **le previsioni generali**, **il bolletino neve** *snow information* or **il bolletino mare e venti** *sea and wind information*.

Talking about holiday plans

1 **2•14** Listen to the key language:

Dove vai/va/andate ...	Where are you going ... (**tu/lei/voi**)
... in vacanza?	... on holiday?
... quest'anno/quest'estate?	... this year/this summer?
Spero di andare ...	I'm hoping to go ...
Vado/Andiamo ...	I'm going/We're going ...
Non vedo l'ora!	I can't wait!
Beati voi!	Lucky you!

2 **2•15** As part of a **sondaggio** *survey*, people are asked where they're going on holiday this year. Read the list of replies given by those holidaying in Italy, then listen and tick the five you hear.

- Vado al mare con la mia ragazza.
- All'Isola d'Elba con la famiglia. Non vedo l'ora.
- Spero di andare in Sardegna.
- Andiamo in montagna in Alto Adige.
- Quest'anno resto a casa.
- Quest'estate vado da mia zia, che abita vicino a Sorrento.
- Vado a Rimini con amici.
- Andiamo in Emilia-Romagna. Mio fratello ha un rustico a quindici chilometri da Modena.

In italiano

Andare *to go* is a key irregular verb:

singular		plural
vado	1st person	andiamo
vai	2nd person	andate
va	3rd person	vanno

G16

3 **2•16** Here's the full reply from one of the people who took part in the **sondaggio** and who's heading off **da sola** *on her own*.
Listen, then fill the gaps with the right form of **andare**.

- Scusi, dove .... in vacanza quest'anno?
- Quest'estate, spero di .... in Sardegna – da sola! Sono divorziata e mia figlia .... in vacanza con il mio ex marito. .... ai Caraibi, dalla nonna.

... and the weather

prevalentemente soleggiato

nebbia

pioggia

parzialmente nuvoloso

nevicate

acquazzoni

nuvoloso

vento forte

temporali

Fa (from **fare**) has more than one meaning.

- It can mean *ago*: **due anni fa** *two years ago*.
- **Fa**, and also **che** *what*, are widely used when discussing the weather:

Fa bello/Che bel tempo! *It's lovely/What wonderful weather!*
Fa brutto/Che brutto tempo! *The weather's awful.*
Fa (molto) caldo/Che caldo! *It's (very) hot.*
Fa 40 gradi all'ombra. *It's 40 degrees in the shade.*
Fa (così) freddo oggi. *It's (so) cold today.*

When saying what the weather was like at a specific time in the past, you replace **fa** with **ha fatto**: **ha fatto bello ieri**.

In italiano

---

4   **2•17** Sergio, who's going to Alto Adige, talks about the weather there. Listen, then make a note under these two headings of what he says about it. And see if you can catch what the average temperature is in July and August. Degrees are **gradi**.

d'estate *in summer*

....

....

d'inverno *in winter*

....

....

In luglio e agosto, la temperatura media è ...... gradi.

Talking about previous holidays

1   **2•18** Listen to the key language:

Dove sei, Dov'è andato/a ...	Where did you go ... (**tu, lei**)
Dove siete andati/e ...	Where did you go ... (**voi**)
... l'anno scorso?	... last year?
Sono andato/a ...	I (m/f) went ...
Siamo andati/e ...	We (m/f) went ...

2   **2•19** As part of the same survey, people were asked where they went on holiday last year. Before you listen, read these replies and anticipate whether they're male or female and whether they are talking about just themselves or more than one person.

   Sono andata al mare.

   Sono andato in Abruzzo, come ogni anno. Mi piace fare trekking.

   Sono andato in Croazia, più precisamente a Zagabria.

   Siamo andate in Sicilia, a Siracusa. Ha fatto molto caldo.

   Sono andata da mia nonna in Inghilterra.

   L'anno scorso non siamo andati in vacanza. I nostri amici australiani sono venuti in Italia.

In italiano

You form the perfect tense of andare, and a few other verbs, with essere, not avere. Most of them relate to movement, e.g. arrivare *to arrive*, venire *to come*, partire *to depart*.

With these essere verbs, the ending of the past participle changes to agree with the subject:

io (m) sono andato	io (f) sono andata
Salvatore è partito	Anna è partita
noi (m) siamo arrivati	noi (f) siamo arrivate
i figli sono andati	le figlie sono andate **G24**

3   In Italian, how would:

   a   a man say *I went to Sicily with my girlfriend*?

   b   two women say *We went to the Caribbean last year*?

   c   a couple say *We went to England with friends*?

   d   a man ask a woman *Did you go to Rome yesterday*?

... and describing what happened

4 **2•20** Listen to the key language:

Ti sei divertito/a?	Did you (m/f) have a good time?
È stato stupendo.	It was superb.
Cos'hai fatto di bello?	What did you do that was nice?
Sei mai stato a Capri?	Have you ever been to Capri?
Non ci sono mai stato.	I've never been there.

5 **2•21** Salvatore's back at work after a holiday. Listen as a colleague asks him about it and try to catch where he went and who he went with.

Dove? .... **Con chi?** ....

Other verbs that form the perfect tense with **essere** are:

- **essere** *to be* (pp stato): Sei stato a Capri?
- **salire** *to come up/go up/get on*: sono salito in autobus
- **scendere** *to come down/go down/get off a train or bus* (pp sceso): sono sceso a piedi
- all reflexive verbs, e.g. **divertirsi** *to enjoy oneself*: mi sono divertito; ti sei divertito?

G24

In italiano

6 **2•22** Salvatore goes on to describe a memorable day on the island of Capri. Before you listen, read the jumbled-up version of events and number them in the order you predict the events occurred.

   a Abbiamo mangiato dei favolosi spaghetti ai frutti di mare.
   b Siamo partiti da Sorrento in traghetto.
   c Siamo scesi a piedi – ottocento scalini!
   d Siamo saliti ad Anacapri in autobus.
   e Verso mezzogiorno siamo arrivati a Marina Grande.
   f Abbiamo passeggiato un po' per le stradine.
   g Siamo tornati a Sorrento verso le sette di sera.
   h Abbiamo trovato un piccolo ristorante.
   i Giovedì siamo andati a Capri.

put it all together

1   Match the picture with the description of the weather.

1 Che brutto tempo!
2 Fa caldo.
3 Fa bello.
4 È nuvoloso.
5 Fa freddo.
6 Ci sono nevicate.

2   Fill the gaps with the right part of the present tense of **andare**.

a Tu, dove .... in vacanza quest'anno?
b Noi .... negli Stati Uniti.
c Voi .... in macchina o in treno?
d Domani io .... a Roma.
e Stefano e Anna .... in montagna.
f Quando .... al mare lei?
g Quest'estate Olivia .... in Sicilia.
h Io .... da sola.
i Spero di .... oggi pomeriggio.

3   Rewrite this passage as if you were Salvatore and it happened two years ago (**due anni fa**) instead of this year.

**Quest'anno vado in vacanza con amici in Sardegna.
Partiamo in traghetto da Genova e arriviamo a Porto Torres.**

4   **Dove va in vacanza?** Give these replies:

a you're going to the seaside by yourself;
b you (and somebody else) are going to Croatia with friends;
c you're going to the Isle of Elba with the family;
d you (and somebody else) aren't going on holiday this year, you're staying at home.

1 **2•23** An Italian friend planning to come over to the UK rings you to ask what the weather's like.

- **Dimmi, che tempo fa oggi?**
- ◆ Tell him the weather's good, that there's sunshine.
- **Fa freddo?**
- ◆ Say no, it's 19°.

2 **2•24** Now to talk about holidays – first, some questions about your plans.

a
- **Dove vai in vacanza quest'anno?**
- ◆ Say you're going to the seaside.
- **Vai da solo/a?**
- ◆ Say no, you're going with friends.

b
- **Lei va in Italia quest'estate?**
- ◆ Say yes, you're hoping to go to Abruzzo with your partner.
- **Una bella regione. Andate in montagna?**
- ◆ Say yes and explain that your **cugino** *cousin* has a house near Roccaraso.
- **Beati voi! Ci sono stato due anni fa.**

3 **2•25** And now some questions about last year's holiday.

- **È mai stato in Italia?**
- ◆ Say you went to Venice last year. Add that you went with friends.
- **Vi siete divertiti?**
- ◆ Say it was superb.
- **Che tempo ha fatto?**
- ◆ Say it was very hot, 35°.

4 How would you reply to these questions?

- **Dove va in vacanza quest'anno?**
- **Dov'è andato/a in vacanza l'anno scorso?**

quiz

1 What's a **settimana bianca**?

2 Which is the odd one out: **Capri**, **Elba**, **Sardegna**, **Sicilia**, **Sorrento**?

3 To ask a friend where he/she's going on holiday, do you need **vado**, **vai**, **va** or **vanno**?

4 Can you think of two verbs beginning with **a** that use **essere** to form the perfect tense?

5 **Sceso** is the irregular past participle of which verb? What does it mean?

6 How do you say in Italian that the weather's dreadful?

7 What's the difference between **fa caldo** and **ha fatto caldo**?

8 Given that **cadere** *to fall* uses **essere** to form the past, how would you say *I fell*?

Now check whether you can ...

- use **andare** to say where you and other people are going
- talk about holiday plans: where you're going and who with
- say you're hoping to go somewhere
- talk about past holidays: say where you went and describe what you did
- comment on the weather

Now that you know how to talk about the past, you could either keep a simple diary in Italian or talk (to yourself or anyone who'll listen and understand) about what you've been doing. Keep it simple and repetitive at first, using **sono andato/a** and linking this and **partire**, **arrivare**, **tornare**, **uscire** with places. Then add detail, such as the time, what you saw, who you talked to and what the weather was like, using **ha fatto**.

Non sto bene

saying how you're feeling

... and describing symptoms

following instructions

choosing alternative solutions

In Italia ...

medico and **dottore** both mean *doctor*. You address him or her as **Dottore** – but you'll also hear a lot of people other than medical doctors being addressed as **Dottore** or **Dottoressa**, since until recently this title was conferred to graduates in all disciplines.

EU citizens can make use of Italy's **Servizio Sanitario Nazionale** *National Health Service* provided they have a European Health Insurance Card (EHIC). In an emergency, the number to dial is 118 and the place to head for is the **Pronto Soccorso** *casualty department* of the nearest **ospedale** *hospital*.

Saying how you're feeling

1 2•26 Listen to the key language:

Cos'hai?	What's the matter with you?
Cos'è successo?	What (has) happened?
C'è stato un incidente?	Has there been an accident?
Sto bene/male.	I'm well/ill.
Mi sento malissimo.	I feel dreadful.
Non riesco a camminare.	I can't (manage to) walk.
Poverino/a!	(You) Poor thing!

2 Read this e-mail from Simona to her friend Amelia. Why can't she meet her at lunchtime?

Da: Simona Cesaretti   **Inviato:** lunedì 3 settembre, 09.30
A: Amelia   **Oggetto:** non sto bene!!!
----
ciao, non posso incontrarti a mezzogiorno perché non vado al lavoro oggi. sto male. mi dispiace. baci, Simona

Stare is used to talk about a person's state of health:
Come stai/sta/state? *How are you?* (tu/lei/voi)
Sto male. *I'm ill.* **Sta meglio/bene.** *He/She's better/well.*

G16

3 2•27 Listen as Amelia rings Simona to find out what's wrong with her then fill the gaps in this part of their conversation.

- **Non .... a camminare. Ahia! Amelia, sto così male.**
- ◆ **Poverina! Ma cos'è ....? C'è stato un incidente?**
- **Un incidente? No. Ieri sono uscita con Lorenzo. .... andati in campagna e .... camminato almeno cento chilometri.**
- ◆ **Simona, non esagerare!**
- **Beh almeno dieci chilometri. E sono ....**

4 E-mail Gianpietro, a mutual friend, explaining that Simona's not going into work today; she's not feeling well because she went to the country with Lorenzo yesterday and fell.

... and describing symptoms

la testa — l'orecchio — la spalla
l'occhio — la schiena
il naso — il braccio
la mano
la bocca — il dito
la caviglia
la gola
il piede
la gamba — il ginocchio

The words for some parts of the body are particularly irregular:
la mano is feminine despite ending in **-o**; the plurals of **il braccio**, **il dito** and **il ginocchio** (m) are **le braccia**, **le dita** and **le ginocchia** (f).

To say something's hurting you can use:
- **avere mal**: Ho mal di testa. *I've got a headache.*
- **fare male**:
Mi fa male il ginocchio. *My knee hurts* (literally, *it hurts me the knee*).
Mi fanno male le ginocchia. *My knees hurt.*
Ti/Le fa male la mano? *Does your hand hurt?* (tu/lei)
Gli/Le fa male il ginocchio. *His/Her knee hurts.*
Note that you don't use the words for *my, your,* etc.

In italiano

G35

---

5 **2•28** Amelia rings Simona again later. Listen and decide which parts of her are hurting.

6 **2•29** Simona then rings her sister Carla, whose response is to say **Non posso chiacchierare** *I can't chat*, because her little boy Luca is ill. Read this list of potential symptoms, listen to Carla, then tick off the ones Luca's displaying from the list.

- gli fa male la bocca
- gli fa male il naso
- gli fa male la schiena
- gli fanno male le braccia
- gli fanno male le spalle
- gli fanno male gli occhi

- ha mal d'orecchio
- ha mal di testa
- ha mal di gola
- ha mal di stomaco
- ha la febbre *temperature*
- ha la tosse *cough*

Following instructions

1 2•30 Listen to the key language:

Mi sono slogato ...	I've sprained ...
Riesce a piegarlo?	Can you manage to bend it?
Prenda un antidolorifico.	Take a painkiller.
Si riposi ...	Rest ...
Faccia ...	Do ...
Fra due giorni ...	In two days' time ...
... tutto sarà a posto.	... all will be back to normal.

2 2•31 A couple of days later, Simona hobbles to the doctor's. Here's an outline of their conversation for you to read with the aid of the glossary before you listen to it.

Her diagnosis:	**Mi sono slogata il ginocchio.**
His diagnosis:	**Un po' contuso. Niente di grave.**
His advice:	**Prenda un antidolorifico, si riposi e faccia un po' di esercizio leggero.**
His prognosis:	**Fra due o tre giorni, tutto sarà a posto.**

In italiano

Prenda *take*, si riposi *rest* and faccia *do* are imperatives, a form of the verb used to give instructions, in this case, to one person (**lei**). The same meaning can be conveyed using **deve** and the infinitive:

deve prendere un antidolorifico
deve riposarsi
deve fare esercizio

G28

3 2•32 Simona goes to the **farmacia** for some painkillers. Listen and see if you can pick out any of the **farmacista**'s instructions, based on what you might expect to hear in English in the same circumstances. Then check with the transcript on page 121.

Choosing alternative solutions

MEDICINA OLISTICA
Mettere in armonia le dimensioni fisiche, emotive, spirituali e sociali della persona

Marco Adone
Allenatore personale
- Stanco/a di allenarti senza risultati?
- Hai problemi con l'alimentazione?

A TUA DISPOSIZIONE LA MIA ESPERIENZA DI MOLTI ANNI

AGOPUNTURA:
ANTICA PRATICA MEDICA CINESE.

Può trattare dolori, artrite, malattie della pelle, disturbi mestruali e della gravidanza.

SHIATSU
Corso on-line per imparare l'arte del massaggio giapponese

SEI STRESSATO?
SEI TESO?
UNA GUIDA PER IL BENESSERE INTERIORE: MEDITAZIONE, ASTROLOGIA E COACHING OLISTICO.

OMEOPATIA

Corsi, seminari, notizie.

Vuoi dimagrire?
Scegli una dieta bilanciata e personalizzata.
Consulenza gratuita via e-mail.

1 Without the help of the glossary, have a look at these adverts taken from the notice board at the chemist's and see if you can find the Italian for: acupuncture, balanced diet, harmony, holistic medicine, homeopathy, inner well-being, massage, personal trainer, stressed.

put it all together

1   Find the odd one out in each line.

   a   caviglia, occhio, orecchio, bocca
   b   meditazione, allenatore, agopuntura, omeopatia
   c   stressato, teso, stanco, soccorso
   d   braccia, testa, spalle, ginocchia

2   Choose the correct ending for each sentence.

a	Giovanna ha	1	malissimo.
b	Non riesco	2	un incidente.
c	C'è stato	3	a camminare.
d	Luca sta	4	la febbre.
e	Sono	5	camminato ieri.
f	Abbiamo	6	caduti ieri.
g	Siamo	7	caduta ieri.

3   Write an e-mail in Italian to your friend Daniele, telling him

   ● you're sorry but you can't meet him this evening (**stasera**),
   ● you're not well, you've got a temperature, your arms and legs hurt,
   ● Paola's got a sore throat and a headache.

   Also, ask him how he is and whether
   ● he went to work today,
   ● he's seen Ugo.

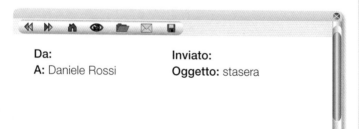

Da: **Inviato:**
A: Daniele Rossi   **Oggetto:** stasera

1 **2•33** Imagine you're Lorenzo, Simona's boyfriend. It's the day after your walk in the country and you've rung her on her mobile.

- Say Hi and ask if she's well.
- ◆ **No, non sto bene. Non sto bene per niente.** (*I'm not at all well.*)
- Ask what the matter is.
- ◆ **Mi fa male la schiena e mi fa male il ginocchio.**
- She clearly needs sympathy. Say *you poor thing* and ask what happened.
- ◆ **Cos'è successo? Ieri è successo!**
- She's not making sense. Ask if she enjoyed herself yesterday.
- ◆ **Lorenzo, ieri abbiamo camminato venti chilometri e oggi non riesco ad alzarmi. Non riesco a ...**
- You need to stop the flow. Tell her the two of you walked five kilometres, then say you've got a lot to do.

2 **2•34** You're now going to describe a whole host of unpleasant symptoms of your own!

- **Come sta oggi?**
- ◆ Say you're not feeling well.
- **Mi dispiace. Cos'ha?**
- ◆ Say you've got a headache and a sore throat.
- **Poverino/a.**
- ◆ And your shoulders hurt.
- **Ha la febbre?**
- ◆ Say yes, and you have a cough and earache.
- **Secondo me, ha l'influenza. Ha preso qualcosa?**
- ◆ Say no but that you want a painkiller.
- **Io ho un prodotto omeopatico molto efficace. Aspetti un attimo ...**

quiz

1 What's the Italian for the casualty department? And the emergency phone number in Italy?

2 What's the difference between **Sto male** and **Sto meglio**?

3 How would you say in Italian that a) your foot hurts and b) your feet hurt?

4 **Agopuntura** and **massaggio shiatsu** – which is **giapponese** and which **cinese**?

5 **Stomaco** means *stomach*, so how do you say in Italian *She's got stomach-ache*?

6 What word is missing here: **non .... a camminare** if you want to say *I can't manage to walk*?

7 Which of these has a different meaning from the other two: **può prendere**; **prenda**; **deve prendere**?

8 What does **Non posso chiacchierare** mean?

Now check whether you can ...

- say how you're feeling
- list simple symptoms
- explain what hurts when you're in pain
- give information on other people's symptoms
- follow straightforward instructions from a doctor or chemist

When you need to say or understand something in Italian, it can help to imagine yourself in similar but English-speaking circumstances and think what you'd expect to hear and have to say.

Ripeta, per favore is a polite way of asking someone to repeat what he or she has just said. Along with words like **allora** *well*, **dunque** or **quindi** *so/therefore*, **comunque** or **però** *however*, it's useful if you find you need some thinking time.

In più 4

1 **Avere o essere?** Fill the gaps.

  a La settimana scorsa io .... scritto una lettera al giornale locale.

  b Mia figlia e mio genero .... comprato una casa a Castelforte sei mesi fa.

  c Negli anni cinquanta io e mio marito .... andati in Australia con i nostri figli.

  d L'anno scorso io .... tornata in Italia.

  e Mi .... sposata due anni dopo la fine della seconda guerra mondiale.

  f Quattro anni fa mio marito .... morto.

  g Mi chiamo Antonia Ferrero; .... nata a Castelforte nel 1928.

  h Ieri il postino .... portato due risposte alla mia lettera.

  i Quindici giorni fa io .... deciso di cercare le mie vecchie compagne di classe.

  j Nel 1981 mia figlia .... venuta a vivere a Roma.

---

decidere (pp **deciso**) *to decide* **il genero** *son-in-law*
una risposta *reply* **scrivere** (pp **scritto**) *to write*
sposarsi *to get married*

---

2 Reveal Antonia Ferrero's life story by arranging the events listed in activity 1 in the order they happened; starting with g. Then write a summary in English.

3 Read about Castelforte and fit in the phrases from the box.

> **il turismo termale** *spa tourism*
> **le terme** *thermal baths*
> **una località termale** *health spa*
> **le proprietà terapeutiche** *therapeutic properties*

Antonia Ferrero abita a Castelforte, ... nel Lazio. ....
sono le antiche Aquae Vescinae, frequentate dai Romani in epoca
imperiale. .... è diffuso in Italia, e molte persone vengono
a *come to* Castelforte per .... delle acque fredde, termali ed
ipertermali che vanno dai 15° ai 69° C.

Venire *to come*, which uses **essere** in the perfect tense, is irregular
in the present tense:

singular		plural	
vengo	1st person	veniamo	
vieni	2nd person	venite	
viene	3rd person	vengono	**G16**

4 Read these replies given during a survey and work out what they mean,
using the glossary only if you get stuck.

Perché è venuto/a a Castelforte lei?
Perché siete venuti/e voi?
- Sono venuta per l'idroterapia, la ginnastica in acqua e il
  massaggio subacqueo.
- Per motivi di salute. Io soffro di asma e vengo qui regolarmente
  perché trovo le acque benefiche.
- Noi veniamo a Castelforte ogni anno per i trattamenti rilassanti.
- Siamo venuti principalmente perché mia moglie soffre d'artrite.
- Le mie amiche, che sono venute l'anno scorso, sono andate pazze
  per i trattamenti estetici.

5 2•35 Now listen to the survey, tick off the reasons as you hear them
and make a note of the last reason you hear, which isn't on the list. It
starts with **Da bambino, venivo ...** *As a child, I used to come ....*

Many adverbs are formed by adding **-mente** to the feminine singular adjective:

chiaro/a *clear* ▸ **chiaramente** *clearly*
semplice *simple* ▸ **semplicemente** *simply*
fortunato/a *fortunate* ▸ **fortunatamente** *fortunately*

In modo is also used with an adjective (m): **in modo responsabile** *responsibly*, **in modo sicuro** *safely*.

G11

6 Read the newspaper cuttings and fill the gaps with an appropriate adverb or phrase from the box below.

veramente	**in modo professionale**	**bene**
evidentemente	**in modo intelligente**	
sfortunatamente	**in modo spettacolare**	

Incidente stradale

Dopo un incidente sulla SS7 nelle prime ore di sabato, una pattuglia della polizia stradale ha trovato una giovane donna coperta di sangue e .... in stato confusionale. "Ha dimenticato tutto, anche il suo nome", il poliziotto ha detto.

I CAMPIONATI EUROPEI

Davide Minelli di Terracina ha sprecato la sua ultima occasione di vincere* una medaglia ai Campionati Europei quando è caduto .... "Sono .... deluso", ha detto Davide ieri, "Ho partecipato a tre campionati e non ho vinto* una medaglia".   *vincere (pp vinto) to win

Una partita di calcio: due punti di vista

I vincitori: "La partita è stata per noi una vittoria stupenda. Per vincere, tutta la squadra deve giocare .... e stasera noi abbiamo giocato .... e siamo stati devastanti. È stato fantastico."
I perdenti: "È un giorno molto triste per noi. Abbiamo giocato .... contro una squadra forte ma .... non è bastato*."   *it wasn't enough

7 Read this letter from Alexis McLeod to a holiday let in Lazio. **Vorrebbe** is the **lui/lei** form of **vorrei**.

> Gentile Signora Pelizza
>
> Ho prenotato una settimana a Villa Terracina dal 21 al 28 aprile. Sfortunatamente devo disdire la prenotazione perché mio figlio, che ha diciassette anni, è caduto ieri durante una partita di calcio e si è rotto la gamba. Chiaramente non posso lasciarlo a casa da solo.
>
> Comunque, un mio amico, il signor Kiel, vorrebbe venire al mio posto e le ha scritto per confermare.
>
> Mi dispiace per il disturbo.
>
> Distinti saluti
>
> A McLeod

a Why is Mrs McLeod cancelling her booking?
b Who is Mr Kiel?

8 Write the letter from John Kiel to Signora Pelizza.

- saying who you are (name and that you're a friend of Mrs McLeod),
- explaining that your friend has cancelled (**disdetto**) her booking and saying why,
- stating you'd like to come to the Villa Terracina in her place, giving the dates.

9 Now write an e-mail from John to his friend Elena in Rome, asking:

- how she is,
- what she did **a Pasqua** at Easter.

and telling her that:

- he went to Scotland,
- it was very cold but he got up early every morning and went walking (**passeggiare**) in the mountains,
- he's coming to Italy in April, giving the dates.
- it's such a long time since they saw each other.

Mi piacerebbe molto

sending an invitation

... and replying

saying what people are like

... and what they look like

In Italia ...

people celebrate not only **compleanni** *birthdays* and **anniversari**
anniversaries, but also festivals like **San Valentino**, **Festa della Mamma**,
Carnevale (the period leading to Lent), and the **Festa della Donna**
(International Women's Day – 8 March), to name but a few. On such
occasions you'll hear the words **auguri** *best wishes* and **buono** *good*: **Buon
Natale** *Happy Christmas*, **Buon compleanno**, **Buone feste**.

When you're invited to something, **galateo** *etiquette* requires a
reply: whether a simple **Grazie** or **Mi dispiace**, a formal **La ringrazio
sinceramente** or **Porgo le mie scuse**, or a minimalist **sms** *text message*
saying **Gra** or **MiDi**.

Sending an invitation

1   Gio, Pascal and Nadia are brainstorming ideas for a **festa**. With the
    help of the glossary, read their suggestions, all with the **noi** form of the
    verb, here meaning *Let's ...* or *Shall we ...*.

Andiamo in un locale notturno.
Mangiamo una pizza.

Invitiamo gli amici per
un aperitivo.
Visitiamo la Cantina Socia
per una degustazione.

Ceniamo all'aperto. Prepariamo una
cena speciale da buongustaio.

What's the Italian for these words: gourmet, outside, wine tasting,
community vineyard and nightclub?

2   As they're on a **corso di cucina** at the Casa Rustica, preparing **una cena
    speciale** wins. Pascal sends invitations to Sofia, whom he has a crush
    on; to Giulia, a friend of Andrea (the head chef); and to Boris, a friend.

1
Cara ....
È invitata a una cena da buongustaio alla Casa Rustica.
Venerdì sera alle otto, festeggiamo il compleanno di Claudia
ad una cena all'aperto, preparata dal gruppo cucina. La prego
di rispondere entro mercoledì.
Saluti, Pascal

2
Ciao ....,
Sei invitato a una cena
speciale per festeggiare
il compleanno di Claudia.
Venerdì sera, alle otto,
sul terrazzo della Casa
Rustica. Fammi sapere
subito se puoi venire.
Pascal

3
Carissima ....
Ti piacerebbe
venire a una cena
specialissima,
preparata da me?
Venerdì sera, alle
otto, alla Casa
Rustica. Vieni. Mi
raccomando. P x

   a Who gets which invitation?
   b When and where is the **cena** to take place?
   c What are the three different phrases Pascal uses to invite?
   d How do you say *by Wednesday* in Italian?

... and replying

3 **2•36** Listen to the key language:

Avrà luogo.	It will take place.
Mi piacerebbe molto.	I'd love to.
Volentieri.	With pleasure.
Mi dispiace ma ...	I'm sorry but ...
Non posso perché ...	I can't because ...
Non so se posso.	I don't know if I can.
Che peccato!	What a pity!

4 **2•37** Gio's job is to phone Feixia, Pedro and Nico. Listen and match the answers to the people. Listen out for **vi piacerebbe**, since Gio's inviting both Nico and Leila.

☐ **Mi dispiace ma venerdì non possiamo. Che peccato!**
☐ **Che bell'idea. Volentieri.**
☐ **Mi piacerebbe molto. Grazie mille.**

5 **2•38** Listen to a message from Enrico and decide why he can't come.

Avere luogo *to take place* is one of several Italian phrases using **avere** which translate into English without necessarily using *have*:

avere fame *to be hungry*   **avere sonno** *to be sleepy*
avere voglia di *to feel like*   **avere paura** *to be afraid*
avere una cotta per *to have a crush on*

Avrà (luogo) is an example of the future tense. More in Unit 10. **G18**

In italiano

---

6 **2•39** Pascal rings Sofia to check she got his text. Listen out for **Hai voglia di venire?** *Do you feel like coming?* Is she coming to the dinner?

Saying what people are like

1 **2•40** Listen to the key language:

Conosci Sofia?	Do you know Sofia?
Non la conosco bene.	I don't know her well.
È davvero simpatico.	He's really nice.
Non (lo) so.	I don't know.
Non (lo) sai?	You don't know?
(Non) sono d'accordo con te.	I (don't) agree with you.

There are two different words for *know*.

- conoscere: to know a person, to be familiar with a thing/place;
- sapere: to know facts. **Sapere** is irregular:

singular		plural
so	1st person	sappiamo
sai	2nd person	sapete
sa	3rd person	sanno

Lo *it* is often included with **sapere** but not translated into English.

2 **2•41** Listen to Pascal and Gio talking about Sofia, then fill the gaps in their conversation with **può**, **so**, **sa**, **sai** and **se** *if*.

G Sofia viene alla cena?
P Non ....
G Non lo ......?
P Ha detto che non .... venire.
G Che antipatica!

3 **2•42** Pascal's devastated after an **sms** from Sofia: **non vengo ve MiDi** *not coming Fri Sorry*. Gio talks to Nadia. Read these adjectives, then listen and note which they use for Pascal and Sofia. Do they agree about Sofia?

allegro *cheerful*	**bravo** *good*
deluso *disappointed*	**divertente** *funny, amusing*
educato *polite*	**gentile** *kind*
maleducato *rude*	**antipatica** *unpleasant*
vanitoso *conceited*	**simpatico** *nice*

... and what they look like

4 2•43 Listen to the key language:

Chi è?	Who is he/she?
Com'è fisicamente?	What does he/she look like?
È snella/in carne.	She's slim/plump.
È mora/bionda.	She's dark/blonde.
È alto un metro e ottanta.	He's 1m 80 tall.
È bello/bella da morire.	He/She's drop-dead gorgeous.

5 2•44 Nadia's doing some subtle matchmaking by talking to Pascal about Gemma from the photography course. Listen and decide

- whether Gemma is ☐ dark ☐ blonde ☐ slim ☐ chubby
- how tall she is.

> *Who* is translated as **chi** when used in a question:
> **Chi è?** *Who is he/she?*
> and **che** when used in a statement:
> **la donna che sorride molto** *the woman who smiles a lot*
>
> **G30**

In italiano

6 2•45 **Capelli** *hair* is plural in Italian. Listen as Nadia carries on chatting to Pascal, and decide:

- whether Gemma's hair is:
  ☐ **lisci** *straight*   ☐ **ricci** *curly*   ☐ **lunghi** *long*   ☐ **corti** *short*
- and whether her eyes are:
  ☐ **azzurri** *blue*   ☐ **marroni** *brown*   ☐ **neri** *black*   ☐ **nocciola** *hazel*

7 2•46 Later Nadia asks Gio whether Boris has replied: **Ha risposto Boris?** Listen, then say in English what Nadia says he looks like. New words are:

> **il tizio basso e grasso** *the short fat bloke*
> **con i baffi** *with a moustache* (like **capelli**, **baffi** is plural)
> **non è né grasso né magro** *he's neither fat nor thin*
> **si veste sportivo** *he dresses casually*

put it all together

1   Make these suggestions in Italian.

  a Let's go to the restaurant.
  b Shall we eat outside?
  c Let's explore!
  d Shall we park here?
  e Let's go to Rome tomorrow.
  f Let's book today and leave at seven o'clock tomorrow.

2   Say what these words mean and give their opposites.

  basso   **corto**   **educato**   **magro**
  biondo   **antipatico**   **snello**

3   Fill the gaps with the words in the box.

  | abbiamo   andiamo   festeggiare   invitati   rispondere |

  > Cari amici,
  > Siete .... a una festa sabato 16 giugno. Per il
  > nostro anniversario di matrimonio, ... organizzato
  > una cena Da Luigi in via Tramontano poi .... al
  > locale notturno in via Veneto.
  > .... entro il 31 maggio per favore.
  > Saluti
  > Rachele e Paolo

4   Write a similar letter to a friend, Salvatore, inviting him to a
    party to celebrate your birthday on Friday October 12th. Tell
    him you've organised a dinner at the Trattoria Pescara at eight
    in the evening, and ask him to reply by September 30th.

5   How would Salvatore reply:

  • thanking you, saying it's a lovely idea and he'd love to come;
  • apologising and saying it's a pity; he can't come because
    he's going on holiday?

1   **2•47** A colleague's telling you about Leona – but you've
     absolutely no idea who she's talking about.

   - **Sai che Leona non è andata al convegno?**
   - ◆ Say you don't know Leona.
   - **Sì, la conosci. Lavora con Giorgio e Lavinia.**
   - ◆ Ask what she looks like; is she tall?
   - **Beh ... non è né alta né bassa. Un metro e sessanta, più o meno. Ha i capelli ricci, gli occhi marroni.**
   - ◆ Ask is she blonde? Thin?
   - **Bionda, sì. E abbastanza snella.**
   - ◆ You've realised who she is. Say yes, you know Leona, she's really nice.
   - **Simpatica? Leona? Secondo me è poco simpatica.** (*She's not very nice.*)

2   **2•48** Your friend Sandro phones to say it's ages since he's seen
     you and to invite you out to celebrate his birthday.

   - **Ciao. Tanto tempo che non ci vediamo! Senti, ti piacerebbe uscire per festeggiare il mio compleanno?**
   - ◆ Say it's a great idea; you'd love to.
   - **Allora, martedì ho organizzato di andare al locale notturno in via Veneto.**
   - ◆ Say you're sorry, you can't on Tuesday because you're going to Milan.
   - **Ah, che peccato! Ma senti, hai voglia di venire ad una festa da Marta? Avrà luogo il tre dicembre.**
   - ◆ Say thanks a lot, you'd love to. Wish him a happy birthday and send best wishes to Marta.

3   **2•49 Com'è fisicamente, Leonardo?** Describe Leonardo,
     who's drop-dead gorgeous: dark-haired, black eyes, 1m 80
     tall, dresses casually.

quiz

1 Which is the odd one out here: **biglietto**, **compleanno**, **auguri**, **baffi**, **festa**, **anniversario**?

2 If you receive a text message saying **MiDi**, what does it mean?

3 What is the Italian for *a wine tasting*?

4 If rich is **ricco** and ultra rich is **straricco**, what do you think **strasimpatico**, **stragrande** and **straordinario** mean?

5 What's the difference in meaning between **la festa ha luogo sabato** and **la festa avrà luogo sabato**?

6 **L'uomo ...... abbiamo invitato**. Is the missing word **che** or **chi**?

7 Would you use **non so** or **non conosco** to say you don't know who's coming to the party?

8 How would you say you feel like doing something: **ho paura**, **ho voglia** or **ho fame**?

Now check whether you can ...

- make a suggestion
- send an invitation
- accept an invitation
- refuse politely, apologising and giving a reason
- describe somebody physically
- describe somebody's character

Put your learning into practice by seeing if you can describe someone, be it your nearest and dearest or someone from a magazine. Double the impact of what you've just learnt by putting **molto**, **un po'**, **piuttosto**, **così**, **proprio** and **abbastanza** *quite* before the adjective. Try comparing people, using **più** and **meno**: **Leona è più alta di Marta** *Leona's taller than Maria*. And if you want to say that someone's the most ..., just add the definite article before **più** and **meno**: **Marta è la più vivace** *Marta's the most lively;* **Giovanni è il più gentile** *Giovanni's the kindest.*

Un vino rosso corposo

following a recipe

choosing wine to complement a dish

commenting on a meal

expressing your appreciation

In Italia ...

you're unlikely to hear someone say they're eating pasta. Rather, they'll specify the type of pasta, such as **tagliatelle**, **tortellini** or **tortelloni**. Eaten with or without a **sugo** *sauce* – fresh pasta is often eaten simply **con burro, sale e pepe**. Fresh or dried, it's always **al dente**, tender outside and firm inside.

Italian wines are known the world over: from the sparkling white Prosecco to the great Barolo and Barbaresco reds. Look out for the label **DOCG: Denominazione di Origine Controllata e Garantita** which guarantees the origin and quality of the wine.

Following a recipe

pentola   coperchio   scodella

padella   cucchiaio

1 These are words often found in recipes:

aggiungere *to add*	**assaggiare** *to taste*
bollire *to boil*	**condire** *to season/dress*
coprire *to cover*	**cuocere** *to cook*
mescolare *to mix/stir*	**mettere** *to put*
scolare *to drain*	**sobbollire** *to simmer*
togliere *to remove*	**versare** *to pour*
il punto di cottura/ebollizione *cooking/boiling point*	

2 2•50 Andrea, **lo chef** at La Casa Rustica, is demonstrating how to cook pasta **in modo corretto**. Listen to his **regole d'oro** *golden rules*, then fill the gaps in this summary (which uses the infinitive where he uses the more informal **noi**). You'll hear him say **cioè** *in other words* a few times.

Cuocere la pasta in modo corretto - le regole d'oro:

a La pentola dev'essere abbastanza grande per contenere almeno un litro d'acqua per ogni .... grammi di pasta.

b .... la pentola con l'acqua su un fuoco alto.

c Al punto di ebollizione, ... poco a poco il sale: circa .... grammi per ogni litro d'acqua.

d Versare la pasta nell'acqua e .... per qualche istante.

e Quando l'acqua riprende il punto di ebollizione, ... il coperchio e mantenere il fuoco alto.

f Durante la cottura .... ogni tanto un pezzettino di pasta. È cotta quando è .... Per la pasta fresca, fatta in casa, ... minuto basta normalmente.

g Al punto di cottura, ... rapidamente la pasta e .... immediatamente in una scodella riscaldata.

h La pasta è più buona se consumata prima possibile.

3 2•50 Listen again – the complete transcript is on page 125. According to Andrea, what are the golden rules for cooking pasta?

Choosing wine to complement a dish

1 **2•51** Listen to the key language:

Abbinare cibo e vino.	To match food and wine.
Viene/Va servito ...	It is/should be served...
... **fresco.**	... chilled.
... **a temperatura ambiente.**	... at room temperature.

2 These are the dishes for the **Cena da buongustaio**. Check the meaning of any new words and label each dish **antipasto**, **primo piatto**, **pesce**, **secondo piatto**, **contorno**, **formaggio**, **frutta** or **dessert**.

> Pecorino sardo
>
> Fagiolini e patate novelle
>
> Frutta fresca e torta al cioccolato e nocciole
>
> Tagliatelle con salsa di cozze e broccoli
>
> Agnello arrosto al rosmarino
>
> Alici fresche
>
> Bruschetta con porcini

3 **2•52** Gio tells Andrea about their choice of wines. Listen and decide which of these wines goes with which course.

Assisi	**Chianti Classico**	**Marsala**
Prosecco	**Torgiano**	**Montepulciano d'Abruzzo**

4 **2•52** Listen again to Gio and Andrea, then label each wine **bianco**, **rosato** *rosé* or **rosso**, and choose one of these adjectives to describe it.

corposo *full-bodied*	**secco** *dry*	**amabile** *medium-sweet*
delicato *delicate*	**dolce** *sweet*	**spumante** *sparkling*
giovane *young*	**intenso** *intense*	**liquoroso** *fortified*
invecchiato *aged*	**leggero** *light*	**robusto** *robust*

È/Sono and **viene/vengono** + past participle both mean *is/are*:

È/Viene servito fresco. *It's served chilled.*

Va/Vanno + past participle mean *should be*:

Va servito fresco. *It should be served chilled.*

In italiano

Commenting on a meal

1 2•53 Listen to the key language:

Ti/Le/Vi è piaciuto?	Did you like (it)?
Mi è piaciuta la torta.	I liked the cake.
Mi sono piaciuti i vini.	I liked the wines.
Perfetto/a!	Perfect!
È cotto/a a perfezione.	It's cooked to perfection.
È un po' dolce/salato per me.	It's a bit sweet/salty for me.
Mi ricorda ...	It reminds me of ...

2 2•54 Before you listen to snatches of conversation heard during the **cena**, see if you can match the two halves of each one.

a **Vuole assaggiare questo vino bianco?**	1 **Mi è piaciuto moltissimo – cotto a perfezione!**
b **È molto robusto questo vino rosso.**	2 **È un po' troppo forte, troppo salato, per me.**
c **Le è piaciuto l'agnello arrosto?**	3 **Perfetta! Non troppo dolce. Secondo me, contiene del rum.**
d **Hai assaggiato il pecorino?**	4 **Mm ... secco, leggero, delicato ... ha un sapore elegante.**
e **Cosa pensi della torta?**	5 **Sì, è davvero corposo.**

3 2•55 Listen to Andrea and his friend Giulia discussing the **torta al cioccolato** and decide who used to make one like it and when. You'll hear **preparava** *used to make* and **serviva** *used to serve*.

Expressing your appreciation

1 2•56 Listen to the key language:

Grazie mille/infinite.	Thank you so much.
Mi fa molto piacere.	It gives me great pleasure.
Complimenti allo/agli chef.	Congratulations to the chef/s.
È andato/a a meraviglia.	It went superbly.
Ci siamo divertiti/e tanto.	We've enjoyed ourselves so much.
Torneremo l'anno prossimo.	We'll come back next year.

2 2•57 At the end of the **cena**, Andrea makes a speech and wishes someone a happy birthday. Listen and pick out:

- what word he uses to describe the **cena**;
- which course he feels was a **capolavoro** *masterpiece*;
- to whom he proposes **un brindisi** *a toast*;
- whose birthday it is.

3 On behalf of the cookery class, Pascal writes a thank-you note to Andrea. Among the **sacco di cose** *pile* (literally, *bag*) *of things* they've learnt, which three are mentioned in the letter?

> Caro Andrea
>
> Grazie mille per tutto. Il corso di cucina è stato meraviglioso, ci siamo divertiti tanto e abbiamo imparato un sacco di cose – non solo come preparare un pasto all'italiana e abbinare cibo e vino, ma anche a parlare meglio l'italiano. Insomma, è stato fantastico. Grazie infinite. All'anno prossimo. Torneremo!
>
> Saluti affettuosi dalla classe del 2007.

In italiano

Verb endings incorporating a distinctive **-r-** sound convey the English *will*. This is called the future tense.

torno *I return*	**tornerò** *I will return*
torniamo *we return*	**torneremo** *we will return*

The full patterns of endings are given on page 137.   **G19**

put it all together

1   Match the words a–j with their meanings 1–10.

a	assaggiare	1	mettere il coperchio
b	compleanno	2	un piccolo pezzo/una piccola parte
c	arrosto	3	fra 5 a 10 gradi
d	spaghetti	4	verdura lunga e verde
e	pezzettino	5	quando il liquido bolle
f	abbinare	6	mangiare o bere una piccola quantità
g	coprire	7	l'anniversario del giorno di nascita
h	fresco	8	un tipo di pasta
i	punto di ebollizione	9	scegliere il complemento
j	fagiolino	10	cotto nel forno

2   Rearrange these instructions to find a recipe for an omelette.

Frittata semplice per due persone.
a   Versate le uova nella padella.
b   Mettetela su un piatto riscaldato.
c   Sbattete le uova con una forchetta.
d   Scaldate 10 grammi di burro in una padella a fuoco alto.
e   Servitela subito.
f   Con una paletta piegate la frittata.
g   Aggiungete sale, pepe e un cucchiaino d'acqua a 4 uova.
h   Lasciate cuocere per 2 minuti.

3   Tick whether these verbs mean *I used to…*, *I am …ing*, or *I will…*

io	imperfect	present	future
comincio			
dormirò			
telefonerò			
andavo			
abito			
lavoravo			
giocavo			
finirò			
avevo			
penso			

now you're talking!

1 **2•58** Take part in the general chatter during a party with neighbours in Italy. You know most of them well enough to use **tu**.

- **Ti piace il risotto?**
- ◆ Say it's excellent – cooked to perfection.
- **Devi assaggiare questo pecorino. È così buono.**
- ◆ Say yes, it's very good, and ask if he's tasted the gorgonzola (m).
- **Il gorgonzola – il mio formaggio preferito! Hm, ma questo è ancora piuttosto giovane … E il vino? Cosa ne pensi?** *What do you think of it?*
- ◆ Comment that it's splendid, so robust and full-bodied. Say you like it.
- **Sono buoni i nostri vini italiani, vero?**
- ◆ Say you really liked the aperitif, the Prosecco.

2 **2•59** You go to talk to your neighbour's grandmother.

- As she's done much of the cooking, say what a beautiful cake.
- ◆ **L'ho fatta io, da una ricetta di mia nonna. Contiene mandorle** *almonds.* **Lei non è allergico alle noci** *nuts*?
- Work out how to say you're not allergic to nuts.
- ◆ **Cosa ne pensa?**
- You taste a piece, say you like it a lot and that it reminds you of a French recipe. Congratulate the chef!
- ◆ **Domani le do la ricetta.**
- It's time to go, so thank your neighbour, Fabrizio, say you've enjoyed yourself so much and say goodbye.

quiz

1 Per ogni cento grammi di pasta, aggiungere un .... d'acqua e 10 grammi di ....

2 What do you think **a fuoco basso** means?

3 Is *to taste* **aggiungere** or **assaggiare**?

4 Which is the odd one out? **Leggero, amabile, robusto, coperchio, corposo.**

5 What's the Italian for *in other words*?

6 Do you think **lavoravano** or **lavoreranno** means *they used to work*?

7 To say a wine should be served at room temperature, would you say **va** or **viene servito a temperatura ambiente**?

8 When you raise your glass, you propose **un** ....

Now check whether you can ...

- understand some of the key words used in recipes
- choose an Italian wine to complement certain foods
- comment on a meal, giving praise or saying what you're not fond of
- say you're allergic to something
- thank your host and express your appreciation
- recognise the verb endings that mean *will* and *was/were/used to*

When you're speaking a new language it's normal to forget words and to be put off your stride as you struggle for the right word. If it happens to you, don't grind to a halt, but try to explain what you want to say using different words. You've seen how this works on page 100 – now have a go yourself at getting round these: **al dente, sobbollire, tagliatelle, prosecco, amabile, splendido, condire.**

In più 5

■ Perugia: la città del cioccolato

L'Umbria, spesso chiamata il cuore verde d'Italia, si trova a tre ore da Roma in treno o in macchina. È una regione piccola che confina a est e a nord-est con le Marche, a ovest e nord-ovest con la Toscana e a sud e sud-ovest con il Lazio. L'Umbria è famosa per i suoi bellissimi paesaggi, i suoi tesori storici, artistici e culturali, i suoi vini … e per il cioccolato.

Fra le più grandi città umbre ci sono Gubbio, Todi, Spoleto e Orvieto. Ma il capoluogo è la splendida città storica di Perugia dove, ogni ottobre, ha luogo la festa del cioccolato. Nel centro storico, nelle piazze e nelle vie ci sono mostre e degustazioni di cioccolato in ogni forma e di ogni gusto.

Le colline umbre sono ideali per la coltivazione di vigne e olivi. I vini umbri, come Orvieto, Torgiano, Montefalco Rosso, Colli Perugini e Colli del Trasimeno, sono di ottima qualità.

1   Vero o falso?

                                                vero   falso

a   L'Umbria si trova nell'Italia centrale. ☐ ☐

b   La Toscana si trova a sud-est dell'Umbria. ☐ ☐

c   Il viaggio in treno da Roma a Perugia dura tre ore. ☐ ☐

d   Gubbio è il capoluogo dell'Umbria. ☐ ☐

e   La festa del cioccolato ha luogo in estate. ☐ ☐

f   La festa del cioccolato ha luogo a Perugia. ☐ ☐

g   Ci sono vigne e olivi nelle colline dell'Umbria. ☐ ☐

h   Colli Perugini è un vino umbro. ☐ ☐

In italiano

There are adjectives relating to regions and towns, for example:

umbro, toscano, siciliano, abruzzese, sardo *Sardinian*
romano, fiorentino, milanese, bolognese, napoletano

People use them to describe themselves, and you're as likely to hear somebody from Rome say **Sono romano** as **Sono italiano**.

2 Rob e Samira Nelson, che abitano vicino a Durham, nel nord-est d'Inghilterra, vogliono scambiare casa con una famiglia umbra. Ecco una descrizione della loro casa.

> **New-build detached house:** hall, cloakroom, sitting room with fireplace + French windows leading to patio, study/4th bedroom, fully equipped family kitchen, utility room. Master bedroom with en-suite, 2 further bedrooms, family bathroom. Gas central heating.
> Double garage, garden to rear with open aspect to golf course.
> Good proximity to shops, schools, station, playground.

Compila questo modulo per i Nelson con ✓ o ✗. Metti un **?** nel caso di mancanza d'informazione *lack of information*.

Paese dove si trova la proprietà	
Tipo di proprietà	
Numero di camere da letto	
Numero di bagni	

Caratteristiche della proprietà			
giardino		box/parcheggio	
terrazzo		vista panoramica	
balcone		piscina privata	
aria condizionata		riscaldamento centrale	

Comfort in dotazione			
cucina moderna		lavastoviglie	
televisione		accesso internet	
ascensore		caminetto	

Prossimità a ...			
negozi		ristoranti	
spiaggia		parco giochi	
piscina pubblica		trasporti pubblici	
palestra		campo da golf	

3 **2•60** Signor e Signora Nelson hanno scambiato casa con la famiglia Marabotti, che abita vicino a Perugia. Loredana Neri abita nella casa accanto *next door*. In questa conversazione con Loredana, tu sei Rob.

- ● Benvenuti in Italia. Io sono Loredana.
- ◆ Say you're pleased to meet her and introduce yourself. Tell her your wife's not here, she's gone into town.
- ● Sua moglie, come si chiama?
- ◆ Answer her question.
- ● Le piace l'Umbria?
- ◆ Say you like it a lot – it's so beautiful and interesting.
- ● È il vostro primo soggiorno in Italia?
- ◆ Say you (i.e. both of you) came to Rome two years ago. Last year you went to France – but you prefer Italy. Add that you personally are crazy about Italy; you've been studying Italian for two years.

2•61 Una settimana dopo, Loredana invita i Nelson a cena.

- ● Allora, che cosa avete visto nella regione?
- ◆ Say that on Monday – on your own – you went to Perugia where you saw the Palazzo dei Priori. You really liked it.
- ● Che tempo ha fatto?
- ◆ Say it was hot.
- ● A che ora è andato?
- ◆ Tell her you left at eight o'clock in the morning.
- ● E cos'avete fatto martedì?
- ◆ Say you (both) went to Arezzo, where you visited the museum.
- ● Avete visto lo splendido Duomo?
- ◆ Say yes, you saw it but, unfortunately, you have no photos because you lost your **macchina fotografica** *camera*.
- ● Che peccato! Avete fatto una denuncia?
- ◆ Say yes, you went to the police station in Perugia.
- ● Un altro bicchiere di vino, Rob?
- ◆ It's getting late, so say 'no, thank you'. Say you've enjoyed yourselves very much but you have to leave. Thank Loredana.
- ● Prego. All'anno prossimo!

4   As if you were Samira, write a card to your friend Mariella in Rome, using your diary as a prompt. Finish off by saying it's been wonderful and you'll be back in Italy next year.

Sat	Arrived Italy, staying (**stare**) in big detached house near Perugia. Supermarket nearby + small trattoria.
Sun	V. hot; R & I got up early and went to Foligno.
Mon	R went to Perugia, saw Palazzo dei Priori. I bought a pile of things at the market!
Tue	Fantastic view here. However, no photos: today p.m. R lost camera. Reported it at police station, filled in form. Then went the wrong way and got back after midnight!

Carissima Mariella,

Bacioni
Samira

Bravo! You've completed *Talk Italian 2* and should now have a broad enough grasp of the structures of Italian to cope in everyday situations without being restricted to set phrases.

Don't expect to remember everything you've learnt. Many people find they need to revisit things several times before they really sink in. So go back occasionally, reading and listening to the units again.

The one really important thing to do is to *use* your Italian. Whenever you can, talk to people in Italian, listen to Italian, read anything you can lay your hands on and write things down.

transcripts and answers

Unit 1
Page 8 Getting to know people

2 ◆ Diamoci del tu.
  ● Come ti chiami?
  ◆ Mi chiamo **Lucia Baldoni**.
  ● Sei italiana?
  ◆ Sì, certo.
  ● Dove abiti?
  ◆ Abito **in centro città** con la mia famiglia.
  Her name is Lucia; she lives in the town centre.

3 ● Ciao, **mi** chiamo Jack.
  ◆ Piacere Jack. **Sei** inglese? Americano?
  ● **Sono** irlandese. Tu, come **ti** chiami?
  ◆ Angelika.
  ● Di dove **sei**?
  ◆ Sono **di** Lodz in Polonia, **sono** polacca. Ma **abito** in Germania.
  ● E io abito **in** Inghilterra, vicino **a** Bristol, con mio fratello.

Page 9 Giving information about people

2 ● Vi presento Angelika. È polacca, di Lodz in Polonia. Abita in Germania.
  ● Si chiama Jack. È irlandese, ma non abita in Irlanda – lui e suo fratello abitano in Inghilterra, vicino a Bristol.

3 ● Sei sposata?
  ◆ **Sì**. Mio marito si chiama **Luciano**. Lucia e Luciano!
  ● Hai figli?
  ◆ Sì, **due**. Si chiamano Marco e **Laura**.
  ● Quanti anni ha?
  ◆ Io? Ma ... questo è un segreto!
  ● No, no, no ... quanti anni ha Laura?
  ◆ Ah – quanti anni ha Laura. Quattro, **ha quattro anni**.
  a vero; b falso, Suo marito si chiama Luciano; c falso, Hanno due figli; d falso, Sua figlia si chiama Laura; e falso, Sua figlia ha quattro anni.

Page 10 Talking about work

2 ● Che lavoro fai?
  ◆ Lavoro nel settore turistico; **organizzo escursioni**.
  ● Che lavoro fai tu?
  ◆ Sono **idraulico**.
  ● Che lavoro fa lei?
  ◆ Sono **illustratrice**. Lavoro da casa.
  ● E tu?
  ◆ Sono **programmatore**, ma attualmente faccio il **cameriere**.
  *There is no **infermiere/infermiera** (nurse).*

3 a Lavoro per il governo, faccio l'addetta stampa **dal 2002**.
  b Faccio l'agente immobiliare **da tredici** (13) **anni**.

Page 11 Explaining why you're learning Italian

2 ● Perché vuoi imparare l'italiano?
  ◆ Perché mi piacciono le lingue.
  ● E tu?
  ◆ Vorrei lavorare in Italia.
  ● Tu, Anna?
  ◆ Per comunicare con la fidanzata di mio figlio.
  ● E tu, perché sei qui?
  ◆ Mi piace la cultura italiana.
  ● Tu?
  ◆ Io? Vado pazzo per l'Italia!
  ● Perché vuoi imparare tu?
  ◆ Mi piacciono la cucina e i vini italiani.
  ◆ Perché la musica lirica è la mia passione.
  ◆ Per curiosità – e basta!
  *a 6; b 2; c 8; d 5; e 4; f 9; g 3; h 7; i 1; **Mi piace molto viaggiare** is not mentioned.*

3 ● Anna, perché vuoi imparare
l'italiano tu?
   ◆ Per comunicare con la fidanzata di
   mio figlio. È italiana.
   ● Di dov'è?
   ◆ Di **Firenze**. Si chiama **Francesca**.
   *Her name is Francesca and she's from
   Florence.*

Page 12 Put it all together

1 *a* 7; *b* 6; *c* 5; *d* 2; *e* 1; *f* 4; *g* 3

2 parlo, parli, parla, parlano
leggo, leggi, legge, leggono
dormo, dormi, dorme, dormono.

3 *a* Mi chiamo Roberto Gallo. Ho
trentadue anni e sono italiano.
Abito a Napoli da quindici anni;
faccio il grafico da otto anni.
   b Vi presento Roberto Gallo. Ha
   trentadue anni ed è italiano. Abita a
   Napoli da quindici anni; fa il grafico
   da otto anni.

Page 13 Now you're talking!

1 ● Ciao! Come ti chiami?
   ◆ **Mi chiamo Rachel Cavanagh.**
   ● Sei americana, vero?
   ◆ **No, sono inglese.**
   ● Di dove sei in Inghilterra?
   ◆ **Di Cambridge.**
   ● Che lavoro fai?
   ◆ **Sono scienziata.**
   ● Da quanto tempo sei scienziata?
   ◆ **Da sette anni.**
   ● Perché vuoi imparare l'italiano?
   ◆ **Perché mi piace viaggiare e vorrei
   lavorare in Italia.**

2 ● **Ciao, come ti chiami?**
   ◆ Lorenzo – Lorenzo Bruno. Piacere.
   ● **Di dove sei?**
   ◆ Sono di Milano.
   ● **Abiti a Milano?**
   ◆ No. Abito a Perugia da tre anni …
   dal duemilaquattro, quando mi
   sono sposato.
   ● **Che lavoro fai?**

   ◆ Sono grafico. Lavoro da casa
   perché ho una bambina piccola.
   ● **Quanti anni ha?**
   ◆ Ha quattordici mesi. È proprio
   bellina.

Page 14 Quiz

*1 using tu; 2 vi presento Giorgio; 3 o;
4 ha; 5 Polonia; 6 dal; 7 mi piace;
8 opera.*

Unit 2

Pages 16 & 17 Using the 24-hour clock and the 12-hour clock

2 ● C'è un volo per Bari che parte alle
diciassette e venti. Comunque
è pieno, non c'è nessun posto
disponibile.
   ◆ E il prossimo volo?
   ● Il prossimo parte alle **diciannove
   e trenta** e ce n'è un altro alle
   ventuno e quattordici.
   ◆ Non c'è un volo prima delle
   diciassette?
   ● No, signore.
   17.20; 19.30; 21.14

3 ● Risponde la segreteria di
Alessandro Pardo. Lasciate un
messaggio dopo il bip.
   ◆ Buongiorno, signor Pardo. Sono
   Jorge Chavez. Il mio volo arriva a
   Bari alle **venti e trentacinque**.
   20.35

4 ◆ Scusi per la confusione, ma arrivo
alle diciotto e venticinque.

5 Signor Chavez, ho appuntamenti
dalle 16.00 **alle** 18.30. Mi chiami
dall'aeroporto di Bari. A più tardi.

7 ● **Cominciamo** alle dieci e un quarto
con il discorso del Ministro sul
cambiamento climatico.
Alle undici meno un quarto
incontriamo gli altri delegati
europei e **scambiamo** informazioni.
Alle undici e mezzo **facciamo** una

pausa per il caffè, poi **riprendiamo** fino al pranzo all'una.
Dopo pranzo, c'è un po' di relax fino alle sette di sera quando ci riuniamo per l'aperitivo. **Ceniamo** insieme alle otto e mezzo.

Pages 18 & 19 Talking about daily routine and the working day

2 a Mi sveglio alle sette. *wake up*
   b Mi alzo alle sette e mezzo. *get up*
   c Di solito mi sveglio alle otto. *wake up*
   d Mi sveglio alle sette meno un quarto. *wake up*
   e Mi alzo alle nove meno dieci. *get up*
   f Qualche volta mi sveglio presto, verso le sei e mezzo. *wake up*

3 ● Mi sveglio presto – verso le sei e mezzo e di solito mi alzo alle sette. Dopo il lavoro, mi alleno – c'è una palestra vicino al mio ufficio – poi mi faccio la doccia e torno a casa per la cena.
   a He gets up at seven; b after work trains at the gym near his office; c showers, goes home to have dinner.

5 ● Monica, a che ora ti svegli?
   ◆ Alessandro ed io, ci svegliamo presto, verso le sei e mezzo. Alessandro si alza alle sette, io invece mi alzo alle otto. Lavoro da casa – sono web designer – ma Alessandro fa il pendolare, lavora a Roma. Esce di casa alle sette e venticinque. La sera, Alessandro va in palestra per allenarsi. Torna a casa, poi ceniamo alle otto, le otto e un quarto.
   Mi sveglio presto (A&M); Mi alzo alle 8 (M); Mi alzo alle 7 (A); Lavoro da casa (M); Sono web designer (M); Faccio il pendolare (A); Esco di casa alle 07.25 (A); Vado in palestra la sera (A); Mi alleno (A); Torno a casa (A); Ceno alle otto e un quarto (A&M).

Page 20 Put it all together

1 *a* 4; *b* 5; *c* 7; *d* 6; *e* 2; *f* 1; *g* 3

2 *b* alle otto di sera; *c* alle quattro e un quarto di pomeriggio; *d* alle sei e venti di mattina; *e* alle undici di sera.

3 *a* lavora; *b* comincia; *c* lavoriamo; *d* ci alziamo; *e* mi alleno; *f* mi alzo.

4 Di solito mi sveglio presto poi mi alzo alle sette e mezzo, esco di casa alle otto e vado al lavoro; torno a casa alle sette di sera, leggo il giornale o guardo la televisione, ceno, qualche volta vado a letto alle undici.

Page 21 Now you're talking!

1 ● Dan, dove abiti?
   ◆ **Abito nel Cheshire.**
   ● Ma lavori a Manchester, vero?
   ◆ **Sì, faccio il pendolare.**
   ● Di solito a che ora ti alzi?
   ◆ **Di solito mi sveglio alle sette e mi alzo alle sette e dieci.**
   ● E a che ora esci di casa?
   ◆ **Esco alle sette e mezzo.**

2 ● Sarah, a che ora si alza Dan?
   ◆ **Si alza alle sette e dieci.**
   ● Dove lavora?
   ◆ **Lavora a Manchester. Esce di casa alle sette e mezzo.**
   ● Sarah, ti piace l'aerobica, vero?
   ◆ **Sì, mi alleno in palestra.**
   ● La sera, mangiate insieme?
   ◆ **Sì, mangiamo insieme a casa.**
   ● A che ora cenate?
   ◆ **Di solito mangiamo alle sette di sera.**

Page 22 Quiz

1 15.35 or 3.35pm; 2 presto;
3 climate change; 4 settantadue;
5 ci; 6 partiamo alle cinque e mezzo e arriviamo alle sette; 7 fa la pendolare;
8 both are from uscire, to go out:
esce = he/she goes out, you (lei) go out;
usciamo = we go out.

In più 1

Pages 23-26

1 **E** Sei tu Simona?

S Enzo! È da tanto tempo che non ci vediamo! Dove **abiti** adesso?

E Qui a Bologna, da quasi tre mesi. **Abito** in via Savanella. I miei genitori **abitano** in periferia come sempre.

S Anche tua sorella Laura **abita** in Emilia-Romagna, vero?

E Sì, sì. Lei e Stefano **abitano** a Sant'Agata, fra Bologna e Modena.

S Stefano **lavora** al museo Lamborghini?

E No, è studente. **Frequenta** l'Università di Bologna; **segue** un corso di Scienze della Comunicazione. **Parla** tre lingue: italiano, inglese e un po' di giapponese.

S E tu, dove **lavori**?

E A Modena. Faccio il pendolare; mi **alzo** alle sei e mezzo e **prendo** il treno delle sette. Che incubo! Ma ogni tanto, quando **lavoro** da casa, mi **alzo** alle dieci! Anche mia moglie si **alza** presto perché i bambini si **svegliano** alle sei ogni giorno.

S Tu hai bambini?! Come si **chiamano**?

2 Di solito nel Regno Unito, le banche aprono alle nove di mattina e chiudono alle quattro di pomeriggio; i negozi aprono alle nove di mattina e chiudono alle cinque e mezzo di sera.

4 *a* BELGIO; *b* IRLANDA; *c* PORTOGALLO; *d* FINLANDIA; *e* GRECIA; *f* ESTONIA
Vado in Belgio; vado in Portogallo; vado in Finlandia; vado in Grecia; vado in Estonia.

5 *a fratello; b suocera; c nipote; d cinque; e Giuseppe; f Giuseppe; g tre; h sorelle.*

6 Mi chiamo Jorge Chavez; sono portoghese. Lavoro a Lisbona, sono scienziato e lavoro per il Centro Conservazione dal 2001. Parlo portoghese, spagnolo, italiano e inglese.
Abito a Cascais in Portogallo e faccio il pendolare. Sono sposato da due anni e ho un figlio. Mi piace molto viaggiare e vorrei lavorare in Brasile.

7 *c* Nico è costruttore dal 2001.
d Ornella è musicista da un anno.
e Francesca è chirurgo da tre anni.
f Valter è idraulico dal 2005.

Unit 3

Pages 28 & 29 Getting local information and advice

2 Guida Enogastronomia – *food and wine guide*; Guida Agriturismo – *Rural tourism guide*; Lista Escursioni Guidate – *Guided tours*; Calendario Eventi e Spettacoli – *Calendar of events and shows*; Cartina della regione – *Map of the region*; Piantina della città – *Town plan*; Elenco ristoranti – *List of restaurants*; Orario apertura del museo – *Museum opening hours*; Guida Sport e Avventura – *Sport and adventure guide*; Lista campeggi – *List of campsites*.

3 ● Buongiorno. Posso aiutarvi?
◆ A che ora apre il museo?
● Ecco **l'orario di apertura**.

◆ Avete una **piantina della città**?
● Sì ... ecco. Prenda anche la **cartina della regione**.

◆ Posso comprare questa **guida sport e avventura**?
● Prego, signora – è gratis. Anche quest'opuscolo.

◆ C'è un buon ristorante qui vicino?
● Ce ne sono tanti. Vi do questo **elenco ristoranti** e la **guida enogastronomia**.

- Posso consigliare Da Luigi, di fronte al castello.
- Si può fare un'**escursione guidata** al lago?
- Sì, ecco una **lista**, con l'orario.
- Possiamo prenotare qui?
- Un attimo... Daniela, puoi telefonare tu all'ufficio?

5&6

- Cosa c'è da fare nella zona?
- Beh, se **vi piace** passeggiare, c'è il sentiero natura (nature walk). Se **preferite** esplorare in macchina (car) – o in bicicletta (bike) – ci sono tantissime cose da vedere. **Potete** visitare la riserva marina (marine reserve) o il castello medioevale (medieval castle), oppure potete **andare** a un vigneto (vineyard). A otto chilometri da qui c'è il nuovo centro di parapendio. No? Beh ... da non mancare se la cultura locale **vi interessa**, sabato c'è la sagra della lumaca (snail festival) a Cavriglia.

Page 30 Talking about leisure interests

2
- Ciao Nico. Dimmi che cosa fai i week-end?
- Vado in piscina, mi piace molto nuotare. E poi ... mi interessa il calcio, sono tifoso della Lazio.
- E tu Luisa, cosa ti piace fare? Ti interessano gli sport?
- Mi interessano gli sport nautici. Sto bene al mare ... mi piace soprattutto fare windsurf.
- Isabella, ti interessano gli sport nautici?
- Assolutamente no. Io preferisco fare kung-fu; mi interessano le arti marziali. Mi piace anche fare trekking con la mia famiglia.
Nico: swimming; football (supports Lazio); Luisa: water sports, windsurfing; Isabella: kung-fu, martial arts, trekking.

3 Ci piace **fare trekking**. Adoriamo la montagna, andiamo spesso in uno dei Parchi Nazionali. Ci interessa **passeggiare lungo i sentieri, essere in contatto con la natura, scoprire paesini caratteristici, ammirare il panorama, godere della pace e del silenzio.**
Ci interessano la flora e la fauna. Nel Parco Nazionale d'Abruzzo si può **osservare l'orso bruno** – un'esperienza incredibile ... da non mancare.

Page 31 Planning an activity

2
- Mi interessa fare un'escursione guidata nella riserva. Si può prenotare qui?
- Non è necessario prenotare. La partenza è qui ogni giorno alle ore nove. L'escursione dura quattro ore. Bisogna indossare scarpe adatte, tipo scarponcini da trekking. Ed è consigliabile portare un maglione o una felpa.
Not mentioned: You need to bring food and water.

3
- Domani andiamo in giro, per esplorare un po'.
- A piedi o in macchina? Oppure potete noleggiare un motorino.
- Esplorare in motorino! Caspita!
The idea of exploring by scooter.

4
- Buongiorno, vorrei noleggiare due biciclette.
- Sì, per quando?
- Per domani mattina, **dalle nove fino a mezzogiorno.**
- Va bene.
- Quanto costa?
- **Una bici costa cinque euro all'ora** o quindici euro al giorno.
- Mi può fare uno sconto?
- **Per due biciclette, no.** Offriamo uno sconto per gruppi di minimo cinque bici.

- Posso pagare con la carta Visa?
- Ma sì, certo. È necessario un documento.

a three hours; b €5 per hour; c no discount offered.

Page 32 Put it all together

1 *a 6; b 4; c 5; d 7; e 3; f 1; g 2*

2 *a ti; b vi; c vi; d le; e ti*

3 I don't have many hobbies. I like to go out with friends, go to town, do some shopping. We particularly like going to the beach at Borgo Marina where we play volleyball and sunbathe. You can go windsurfing but I'm not very good at it.

I am interested in music because my aunt is a singer. And I like dance – I go to a modern dance class every Wednesday. And you? What do you like doing?

Page 33 Now you're talking!

1 ● Buongiorno. Posso aiutarvi?
- **Buongiorno. Avete una guida enogastronomia?**
● Ecco .... con tutti i ristoranti e le trattorie.
- **C'è un buon ristorante qui vicino?**
● Se vi piace la cucina italiana tradizionale, la Trattoria Moretta ha una buona reputazione.
- **Cosa c'è da fare all'Aquila?**
● Ah ... ci sono tante cose da vedere, da fare. Vi do questa guida e un calendario degli eventi.
- **Ci interessa la natura. Si può fare un'escursione guidata nel Parco Nazionale?**
● Nel Parco del Gran Sasso ci sono escursioni a piedi, a cavallo o in mountain bike. Ecco i dettagli. È consigliabile prenotare ... e indossare scarpe comode!
- **Si può noleggiare un motorino qui vicino?**

● Sì, in via Matteotti ... guardi sulla piantina, qui.

2 ◆ **Che cosa fai i week-end?**
● Beh ... un po' di shopping, esco con amici – andiamo al cinema, in discoteca ... mangiamo al ristorante.
◆ **Ti piacciono gli sport?**
● Sì, mi piace nuotare, giocare a pallavolo. Lo sci nautico anche.
◆ **Ti interessa il calcio?**
● Il calcio? Ma senz'altro – sono tifoso della Juventus. Ma dimmi, cosa fai tu nel tempo libero?

3 A bit of shopping, he goes out with friends, to the cinema, nightclub; they eat out.

Page 34 Quiz

1 wine and food; 2 può; 3 vi interessa; 4 you'd wear it – it's a sweatshirt; 5 they all refer to voi; 6 sagra (festival), others all found in tourist office; 7 si può; 8 not to be missed.

Unit 4

Page 36 Reading property descriptions

1 *a* villa indipendente, appartamento, villetta a schiera, rustico, mulino
b bagno, bagno di servizio, camera, cantina, cucina, ingresso, sala da pranzo, salone, soggiorno
c box/garage, giardino, terrazzo
d centralissimo, comodo, collinare, isolato, panoramico, soleggiato, storico, tranquillo

Page 37 Describing a property

2*a* ● Scusi, mi può descrivere la sua casa?
◆ Abito in un **palazzo di nuova costruzione**. Ho un bilocale – piccolo ma è in posizione **centrale** e così **comodo**. Ho il mio balcone. Mi piace.

b ● Signora, signore, mi potete

descrivere la vostra casa?

◆ Noi abitiamo in un **rustico** a venti chilometri da qui. È molto **vecchio** e totalmente ristrutturato. Si trova in una zona **tranquilla**, però non siamo isolati.

c ● Com'è la tua casa?

◆ Vivo con amici. Hanno una villetta, una **villetta a schiera**. Beh … è **moderna**, non c'è giardino e il loro terrazzo è piccolissimo! Comunque, la villetta si trova a tre chilometri dal centro – molto **conveniente** per il lavoro!

3 ◆ Com'è la casa?

● Abbiamo una cucina grande, dove mangiamo – non c'è sala da pranzo – e un soggiorno. Abbiamo tre camere da letto, un bagno e anche un bagno di servizio.

◆ E fuori? Avete un garage?

● Un box, no. Fuori c'è un bellissimo giardino con alberi e fiori, e ha una vista sul Parco Nazionale – il panorama dal terrazzo è stupendo.

three bedrooms; two bathrooms; no garage; superb view of National Park.

Page 38 Enquiring about renting a villa

1 *a three bedrooms, two bathrooms; b 15 minutes; c yes; d nature reserve; e €1050.*

3 ● Pronto.

◆ Buongiorno. Chiamo dall'Inghilterra. Penso di prendere in affitto una casa in Italia in agosto. Mi può dare delle informazioni sulla vostra villa?

● Certo, signora.

◆ Quante camere ci sono?

● Tre camere; otto posti letto. C'è un divano letto nel soggiorno.

◆ E quanti bagni?

● Ce ne sono due, incluso il bagno di servizio al piano terra.

◆ C'è un giardino?

● C'è un giardino dietro la casa. Terrazzo anche.

◆ Si può parcheggiare?

● Sì, c'è il box auto.

◆ C'è la lavastoviglie?

● Sì sì, la cucina è modernissima, totalmente arredata.

◆ La villa è vicino al mare?

● La spiaggia è a due chilometri e c'è anche la piscina municipale.

◆ Quanto costa alla settimana?

● Milleduecento euro.

a three; b two; c yes, behind the house; d yes, there's a garage; e yes; f beach is 2km away; g €1200.

Page 39 Showing someone round a house

2 ● Allora, ecco il soggiorno, con il camino e la finestra con vista panoramica.

◆ Che bella stanza! È **così** spaziosa – e che vista!

● Qui abbiamo la cucina, **molto** spaziosa anche. Tutto è nuovo di quest'anno: il forno, la lavastoviglie, il frigo.

◆ Non c'è la lavatrice?

● Ma sì, si trova nel bagno di servizio. L'asciugabiancheria anche. Ecco le camere, questa con i letti gemelli e questa a sinistra con i letti a castello.

◆ Questa è **un po'** piccola.

● È **piuttosto** compatta, sì. Qui abbiamo la camera principale. E non dimenticate che il divano nel soggiorno è un divano letto. Allora, accomodatevi. Buona permanenza!

3 a trecentomila euro €300.000

b quattrocentocinquantamila euro €450.000

c ottocentoventimila euro €820.000

d quattrocentomila euro €400.000

e novecentocinquantamila euro €950.000

Page 40 Put it all together

1 centrale/isolato; compatto/spazioso;
grande/piccolo; mare/montagna;
nuovo/vecchio; rurale/urbano;
asciugabiancheria/lavatrice.
Cantina cellar, is left over.

2 *a ingresso; b soggiorno; c cucina;
d sala da pranzo; e bagno; f camera
(da letto); g terrazzo; h box/garage*

3 VENDESI Villa, di nuova costruzione,
con vista mare, a cinque minuti dal
mare. Giardino + terrazzo soleggiato.
Tre camere; due bagni.

AFFITASI Rustico spazioso in
posizione panoramica, tranquillo ma
non isolato. Piano terra: ingresso,
soggiorno, cucina attrezzata, bagno di
servizio. Primo piano: quattro camere;
bagno. Giardino grande + box.

Page 41 Now you're talking!

1 ◆ Villa Marina. Pronto.
  ● **Penso di prendere in affitto una
    casa in Italia. Mi può descrivere
    Villa Marina?**
  ◆ È una bellissima villetta con
    giardino e terrazzo.
  ● **È vicino al mare?**
  ◆ Si trova a tre o quattro chilometri
    da una splendida spiaggia.
  ● **Quanto costa alla settimana?**
  ◆ Milletrecento euro.
  ● **Quante camere ci sono?**
  ◆ Ce ne sono tre. Comunque, può
    ospitare fino a nove persone.
  ● **E quanti bagni?**
  ◆ C'è il bagno principale al primo
    piano.
  ● **C'è la lavatrice?**
  ◆ Ma certo.
  ● **C'è la lavastoviglie?**
  ◆ No, non c'è.
  ● **Allora, grazie e arrivederci.**

2 ◆ Com'è la sua casa?
  ● **È un rustico.**
  ◆ Dove si trova?
  ● **Si trova a dieci chilometri da
    Stresa.**
  ◆ È grande la casa? Quante camere ci
    sono?
  ● **Ce ne sono sei.**
  ◆ Sei! E quanti bagni?
  ● **Ce ne sono cinque.**
  ◆ Bello! Avete un giardino?
  ● **C'è un piccolo giardino e un
    terrazzo.**
  ◆ Allora – arrivederci e buona
    permanenza.

Page 42 Quiz

*1 block of flats; 2 needs renovation;
3 un garage; 4 lavatrice; 5 la vostra;
6 Che bella casa; 7 piuttosto; 8 collinare*

In più 2

Pages 43–46

1 *a 3 la Sicilia; b 2 l'Abruzzo;
c 1 la Toscana*

2 *a ✓✓; b ✗✓; c ✓✓; d ?✓; e ??;
f ✓✓; g ✓✓; h ✓✓; i ✓?; j ?✓*

3 Dear Mr Vissani,
I am interested in spending two weeks
at the Torre Vecchia with my wife and
two friends. Can you tell me if it is
available from 22 September until 6
October? Can you confirm the weekly
price for this period, including the use
of a garage?
We would also like to know if there is
a washing machine and if the kitchen
area has a freezer.
Best wishes …

4 Gentile Signor Vissani,
Mi interessa trascorrere una settimana
presso La Torre Vecchia con tre amici.
Mi può dire se è disponibile dal 28
luglio al 4 agosto? Può confermare la

quota settimanale per questo periodo, inclusa l'assicurazione?
Vorremmo anche sapere quante camere ci sono e se c'è una lavastoviglie.
Distinti saluti ...

6 il mio/il suo zaino; la mia/la sua torcia; le mie/le sue scarpe da trekking; il mio/il suo cappello; i miei/i suoi guanti; la mia/la sua giacca impermeabile; i miei/i suoi occhiali da sole.

7 la nostra bussola; il nostro binocolo

Unit 5

Pages 48 & 49 Shopping for clothes, shoes and bags

2a● Cerco una camicia bianca, di lino.
  ◆ Che taglia signore?
  ● Quarantotto.

b ◆ Cerco un paio di jeans. Taglia trentotto.

c ● Signora?
  ◆ Desidero un top nero.
  ● Di cotone? Lana? Seta?
  ◆ Di seta.

d ● Cerco un pantalone grigio.
  ◆ Che taglia?
  ● Quarantasei.

e ◆ Cerco una maglia verde, di pura lana o cachemire. Taglia media, quarantadue o quarantaquattro

f ◆ Posso aiutarla?
  ● Grazie, no. Sto guardando.
  a white linen shirt, size 48; b pair of jeans, size 38; c black silk top; d grey trousers, size 46; e green jumper in pure wool or cashmere, size medium 42-44; f buys nothing, just looking.

3 ◆ Posso aiutarvi?
  ● Cerchiamo una giacca di cotone. Azzurra o blu.
  ◆ Che taglia? È per lei, signora?

● No, è per nostra figlia. Taglia trentaquattro.
◆ Abbiamo questa che costa centoventicinque euro, poi c'è questa qui ....
a cotton jacket; b blue or navy; c their daughter; d €125.

5 ● Vorrei provare questi stivali.
  ◆ Che numero porta?
  ● Trentotto.
  ◆ Mi dispiace ma li abbiamo solo in trentanove o quarantuno. O vorrebbe provarli in nero?
  ● No grazie.
  38; 39 or 41; black.

6 *a* leggero *lightweight;* impermeabile *waterproof;* lavabile *washable;* comodo *comfortable;* capiente *capacious*
  b cerniera; tasca; tasche

7 ◆ Ho comprato questo zaino ma voglio cambiarlo perché la cerniera è rotta.
  ● Posso vederlo, per favore?
  ◆ Questa qui sulla tasca interna.
  the zip's broken; voglio cambiarlo.

Pages 50 & 51 Expressing your opinion and making comparisons

2 **D** Mamma, cosa pensi di questa **giacca**? Mi va bene?
  G Secondo me, è un po' grande. Le maniche sono troppo lunghe.
  S Non mi piace. Secondo me, questa qui ti sta meglio.
  D Susanna, non fare la cretina. Quella lì è troppo vivace. Mamma, questo **pantalone** – è abbastanza lungo? Non è troppo corto?
  G No, è perfetto con quelle **scarpe** nere. Cosa pensi di questa **cravatta**?
  D Boh ... un po' spenta.
  S A me piace questa **cravatta a farfalla**. Con una bella camicia bianca e un **gilet** giallo canarino.

3 **D** Mamma, cosa pensi di **questa** giacca? Mi va bene?

G Secondo me, è un po' grande. Le maniche sono troppo lunghe.

S Non mi piace. Secondo me, **questa** qui ti sta meglio.

D Susanna, non fare la cretina. **Quella** lì è troppo vivace. Mamma, **questo** pantalone – è abbastanza lungo? Non è troppo corto?

G No, è perfetto con **quelle** scarpe nere. Cosa pensi di **questa** cravatta?

D Boh … un po' spenta.

S A me piace **questa** cravatta a farfalla. Con una bella camicia bianca e un gilet giallo canarino.

5 **C** Quale vestito preferisce, signora?

G Il rosso è più pratico.

S Io preferisco il giallo. È più sexy, più stravagante.

G Il giallo è un po' stretto, il rosso è più comodo.

S Mamma, secondo me, il rosso è un po' corto per te.

G È vero, il giallo è più lungo. Ma è carissimo questo giallo – però meno caro del rosso. Mah!

Grazia thinks that the red one's more practical, more comfortable, more expensive; the yellow one's a bit tight, longer and very expensive.

6 **C** Questo vestito è molto **elegante**, signora. È **moderno** e il colore è **bellissimo**.

S Mamma, questo non ti sta bene. È **antiquato** … **preistorico**, e il colore è **orrendo**.

Page 52 Put it all together

1 *a* più, *b* lungo, *c* vivace, *d* interno, *e* bianco, *f* pratico, *g* grande, *h* moderno.

2 *a* Mi sta bene questa giacca bianca?
b Quella cravatta è più spenta.
c Ti piacciono le scarpe nere?
d Preferisci il top verde o il rosso?
e Gli stivali sono un po' grandi.

f Posso provare la maglia con le maniche lunghe?
g Secondo me, lo zaino blu è meno capiente.
h Che pensi del vestito giallo?

3 *a* Li compro a Milano.
b La lavo a mano.
c Posso cambiarlo?
d Voglio pagarli.
e La paga con carta di credito?
f Vorrei provarle.

4 • Cerco un jeans; taglia trentotto.
• Cerco una camicia bianca di lino.
• Cerco una giacca blu di pura lana, taglia quaranta.
• Cerco uno zaino leggero impermeabile, con tasche interne.

Page 53 Now you're talking!

1 • Posso aiutarla?
 ◆ **Cerco una giacca.**
 • Che taglia?
 ◆ **Quarantasei.**
 • Allora. Abbiamo giacche di cotone, lino, viscosa, poliestere, jeans … o forse desidera una giacca di lana?
 ◆ **Sì, vorrei una giacca di lana.**
 • E che colore?
 ◆ **Nero o blu.**
 • Abbiamo questa blu di pura lana vergine, o questa qui di lana con 40% cachemire.
 ◆ **Posso provare la nera?**
 • Si accomodi – è bellissima questa qui.
 ◆ **Quanto costa?**
 • Oh, il prezzo è molto ragionevole, trecentonovanta euro (€390).

2 • C'è un problema?
 ◆ **Sì, questo è rotto, e vorrei cambiarlo.**
 • Posso vederlo?
 ◆ **Qui.**
 • Sfortunatamente non ne abbiamo altri di questo tipo. Le piace questo qui?
 ◆ **Cosa/Che pensi di questo?**

- Secondo me è un po' piccolo.

3 ● Ti piacciono questi? Mi stanno bene?
  ◆ **Secondo me, sono un po' stretti.**
  ● Ma sono così belli. E c'è uno sconto del 25%.
  ◆ **Preferisco questi qui, e sono meno cari.**
  ● Caspita! Sono fantastici.

Page 54 Quiz

1 sto guardando; 2 cerco, cercare, cerchiamo; 3 a) clothes shop, b) shoe shop; 4 emerald green; 5 non mi piace la grigia; 6 della; 7 a me piace emphasises the 'I'; 8 una cerniera.

Unit 6

Pages 56 & 57 Asking the way and following directions

2 ● Scusi signora, ci può aiutare? Dove si trova la questura?
  ◆ La questura è in via Marconi. Siete a piedi?
  ● Sì.
  ◆ Vediamo … **giù di qui fino al semaforo**, girate a destra – no, a sinistra – in via della Vittoria. **Continuate** sempre dritto **in direzione della stazione.** Arrivati al municipio **sulla vostra sinistra, dovete girare** a destra poi **dovete prendere** la terza a sinistra. **Seguite** la strada, **attraversate** la piazza e la questura si trova **lì in fondo**. Avete capito?

3 ◆ Avete capito?
  ● Allora, dobbiamo andare fino al semaforo, girare a sinistra, continuare sempre dritto fino al municipio. Là dobbiamo girare a sinistra poi prendere la terza a sinistra, attraversare la piazza e la questura si trova lì in fondo?
  It should be a right turn (not left) at the town hall.

4 ● Scusi, signora, dov'è il bancomat più vicino?
  ◆ Dunque, al semaforo girate a sinistra e continuate sempre dritto. Poi, se girate a sinistra subito dopo il municipio, in direzione della cattedrale, c'è la banca sulla vostra destra con lo sportello bancomat fuori.
  You end up at A.

6 ● Signore, scusi, è questa la strada per la questura?
  ◆ No, avete sbagliato strada, signora. La questura è in via Marconi – piuttosto lontano da qui. Ma potete prendere l'autobus, Linea settantanove – la fermata è a due passi. Dovete scendere alla stazione e seguire viale Garibaldi. La questura si trova a destra dopo duecento metri. Avete capito?
  a in Via Marconi, rather far; b 79; c very close; d the station; e Viale Garibaldi; f on the right after 200 metres.

Page 58 Explaining what's happened

2 ● Pronto Stefania. Sono Leo.
  ◆ Ciao Leo, ci vediamo alle cinque, vero?
  ● Senti, Stefania, **ho perso** il mio portatile.
  ◆ Come? Cos'**hai detto**? Cos'**hai fatto**?
  ● **Ho detto**: ho smarrito il mio portatile.
  ◆ **Hai fatto** una denuncia? Dovete andare alla questura. Subito.
  ● Sì, chiaro, sì. Oh – Stefania, Roberto **ha telefonato** ieri.
  ◆ Leo – vai! Mi raccomando! Arrivederci.

3 ● Senti Franco. Siamo in ritardo. Abbiamo perso …
  ◆ Abbiamo??
  ● Beh, *io* ho perso il portatile.

*Because it was Leo who lost the laptop,
but he's saying that 'we' lost it.*

Page 59 Reporting a problem

2 cercare *to look for;* compilare *to fill in;*
lasciare *to leave;* appoggiare *to lean,
put down.*

3 A Allora, signore, signora, che cosa è
successo?

  L Abbiamo smarrito il computer
portatile. Oggi, alle dieci, eravamo
all'ufficio postale per inviare
un pacchetto in Inghilterra. Ho
appoggiato il portatile per terra …

  A Signora, lei ha visto il portatile?

  S Sì, l'ho visto.

  L … ho compilato il modulo, ho
pagato, ho messo il portafogli e gli
occhiali in tasca … e poi, quando ho
cercato il portatile, non c'era. L'ho
lasciato solo per un attimo.

  A Basta un attimo, signore. Ha visto
qualcuno vicino?

  L Nessuno.

  A Signora?

  S No, non ho visto nessuno. Non ho
visto niente.

  Order of events: d; b; a; e; c.

4 Ha appoggiato il portatile per terra,
ha compilato il modulo, ha pagato,
ha messo il portafogli e gli occhiali in
tasca, ha cercato il portatile.

5 *a* We've left it at home.
  b Have they seen it?

Page 60 Put it all together

1 *a* Cos'hai detto?
  b Non ho visto nessuno.
  c Non ho visto niente.
  d Cosa è successo?
  e Non ho capito.
  f Cosa avete fatto?

2 *a* Ho smarrito il mio passaporto.
  b Hai visto la mia scarpa?
  c Abbiamo capito il documento.

d Stella ha prenotato l'escursione
  guidata.
e Hai lasciato il telefonino a casa?
f Leo ha appoggiato il portatile per
  terra.
g Ho seguito la strada.
h Ha finito il corso?
i Hanno compilato il modulo.
j Avete visto la villa?

3 *a* L'ho smarrito.
  b L'hai vista?
  c L'abbiamo capito.
  d Stella l'ha prenotata.
  e L'hai lasciato a casa?
  f Leo l'ha appoggiato per terra.
  g L'ho seguita.
  h L'ha finito?
  i L'hanno compilato.
  j L'avete vista?

Page 61 Now you're talking!

1 ● **Scusi signore, ci può aiutare?**
  ◆ Mi dica.
  ● **Dove si trova la questura?**
  ◆ In viale Torricelli.
  ● **Scusi signora. È questa la strada
    per la questura?**
  ◆ Sì, non è lontano. Giù di qui fino
    al semaforo. Lì dovete girare a
    sinistra. Seguite la strada fino a
    via della Vittoria, girate a destra e
    viale Torricelli si trova sulla vostra
    sinistra.
  ● **Ho capito. Grazie.**

2 It's not far. Down here to the lights,
turn left, follow the road as far as Via
della Vittoria, turn right and Viale
Torricelli is on the left.

3 ● Pronto. Paolo Fulvio.
  ◆ **Che cosa è successo?**
  ● Stefano ha …
  ◆ **Cos'hai detto?**
  ● Stefano ha smarrito il suo palmare.
    L'hai visto tu?
  ◆ **L'ho visto ieri. Al ristorante.**
  ● Ha perso tutto – dati,

appuntamenti, numeri di telefono.
È molto stressato.

- ◆ **L'ha lasciato da Franca?**
- ● Può darsi, può darsi. E voi due, cos'avete fatto oggi?
- ◆ **Abbiamo prenotato un viaggio a Venezia.**
- ● E dove avete mangiato?
- ◆ **A mezzogiorno abbiamo mangiato in una trattoria in Piazza Dante.**
- ● Mmm ... bello!

Page 62 Quiz

1 113, questura; 2 very close; 3 if you have understood; 4 qualcosa; 5 have the wrong number; 6 È questa la strada per la stazione?; 7 scendere; 8 ho comprato, ho venduto.

In più 3

Pages 63–66

1 *1* nome: D'Angelo/D'Ancona; *2* nato a Venezia/Verona; *3* residente in via Amalfi 23/piazza Amalfi 26; *4* smarrito il 5/6 marzo; *5* smarrito il pomeriggio/ la mattina; *6* smarrito nel centro sportivo/centro commerciale; *7* portafogli nero/marrone; *8* contenuti €200/300; *9* contenuti patente di guida/passaporto; *10* valore totale €235/€350.

2 *a falso; b falso; c vero; d falso; e vero; f falso; g vero.*

3 l'ha paragonato; l'abbiamo comprata; non l'ho provato; l'ha definito; non le ho comprate.

4 Ieri ho visto una giacca di lana nera che ho provato. L'ho trovata un po' grande ma l'ho comprata. Comunque oggi vorrei cambiarla! Ho anche comprato una camicia bianca e un paio di scarpe nere di pelle – e li ho lasciati nel negozio!

5 bella giacca, bell'appartamento, bel

parco, begli stivali, bella cucina. quelle scarpe, quello zaino, quella regione, quel giardino, quei vestiti.

6 *a* marsupio; *b* guanti; *c* giacca; *d* scarpe da sport; *e* borsetta; *f* borsone da viaggio.

Unit 7

Pages 68 & 69 Talking about holiday plans and the weather

2 ● Dove vai in vacanza quest'anno?
- ◆ **Vado a Rimini con amici.**

- ● E lei, dove va in vacanza quest'anno?
- ◆ **All'Isola d'Elba con la famiglia. Non vedo l'ora.**

- ● Dove andate in vacanza quest'anno?
- ◆ **Andiamo in Emilia-Romagna. Mio fratello ha un rustico a quindici chilometri da Modena.**
- ● Beati voi!

- ● Dove va in vacanza quest'anno?
- ◆ **Quest'estate vado da mia zia, che abita vicino a Sorrento.**

- ● Dove vai in vacanza quest'anno?
- ◆ **Vado al mare con la mia ragazza.**

3 ● Scusi, dove **va** in vacanza quest'anno?
- ◆ Quest'estate, spero di **andare** in Sardegna – da sola! Sono divorziata e mia figlia **va** in vacanza con il mio ex marito. **Vanno** ai Caraibi, dalla nonna.

4 ● E voi, dove andate in vacanza quest'anno?
- ◆ Andiamo in montagna in Alto Adige.
- ● Che tempo fa in Alto Adige?
- ◆ Beh ... d'estate, in luglio e agosto, **fa bel tempo**, **fa caldo**, anche in montagna, con una temperatura media di **23 gradi**. Ma d'inverno ci sono **nevicate** – noi andiamo

per la settimana bianca. Ma anche d'inverno **c'è il sole.**

Pages 70 & 71 Talking about previous holidays and describing what happened

2 ● Ciao. Dove sei andata in vacanza l'anno scorso?
   ◆ **Sono andata al mare.** *(one female)*

   ● Dov'è andato in vacanza l'anno scorso?
   ◆ **Sono andato in Abruzzo, come ogni anno. Mi piace molto fare trekking.** *(one male)*

   ● Signore. L'anno scorso, dove siete andate in vacanza?
   ◆ **Siamo andate in Sicilia, a Siracusa. Ha fatto molto caldo.** *(more than one female)*

   ● Ciao. Dimmi, l'anno scorso dove sei andata in vacanza?
   ◆ **Sono andata da mia nonna in Inghilterra.** *(one female)*

   ● Scusi, dov'è andato in vacanza l'anno scorso?
   ◆ **Sono andato in Croazia, più precisamente a Zagabria.** *(one male)*

   ● Dove siete andati in vacanza l'anno scorso?
   ◆ **L'anno scorso non siamo andati in vacanza. I nostri amici australiani sono venuti in Italia.** *(more than one person)*

3 *a* Sono andato in Sicilia con la mia ragazza.
   b Siamo andate ai Caraibi l'anno scorso.
   c Siamo andati in Inghilterra con amici.
   d Sei andata a Roma ieri?

5 ● Ciao Salvatore. Ti sei divertito?
   ◆ È stato stupendo!

● Cos'hai fatto? Dove sei andato?
◆ **Sono andato alla Baia di Napoli con Francesca,** la mia ragazza. Sei stato a Capri?
● No, non ci sono mai stato.
He went to the Bay of Naples with his girlfriend Francesca.

6 ● Cos'hai fatto di bello?
   ◆ Giovedì siamo andati a Capri. È stato bellissimo. Siamo partiti da Sorrento in traghetto, e verso mezzogiorno siamo arrivati a Marina Grande. Siamo saliti ad Anacapri in autobus. Abbiamo trovato un piccolo ristorante dove abbiamo mangiato dei favolosi spaghetti ai frutti di mare. Dopo pranzo, abbiamo passeggiato un po' per le stradine. Poi, siamo scesi a piedi – ottocento scalini! Siamo tornati a Sorrento verso le sette di sera. È stato stupendo.
   Correct order: i, b, e, d, h, a, f, c, g.

Page 72 Put it all together

1 *a* 3; *b* 5; *c* 6; *d* 4; *e* 2; *f* 1.

2 *a* vai; *b* andiamo; *c* andate; *d* vado; *e* vanno; *f* va; *g* va; *h* vado; *i* andare.

3 Due anni fa sono andato in vacanza con amici in Sardegna. Siamo partiti in traghetto da Genova e siamo arrivati a Porto Torres.

4 *a* Vado al mare da solo/sola.
   b Andiamo in Croazia con amici.
   c Vado all'Isola d'Elba con la famiglia.
   d Non andiamo in vacanza quest'anno; restiamo a casa.

Page 73 Now you're talking!

1 ● Dimmi, che tempo fa oggi?
   ◆ **Fa bel tempo, c'è sole.**
   ● Fa freddo?
   ◆ **No, fa diciannove gradi.**

2*a*● Dove vai in vacanza quest'anno?
   ◆ **Vado al mare.**

- Vai da solo/a?
- No, vado con amici.

b
- Lei va in Italia quest'estate?
- Sì, spero di andare in Abruzzo con il mio partner/la mia partner.
- Una bella regione. Andate in montagna?
- Sì, mio cugino ha una casa vicino a Roccaraso.
- Beati voi! Ci sono stato due anni fa.

3
- È mai stato in Italia?
- Sono andato a Venezia l'anno scorso. Sono andato con amici.
- Vi siete divertiti?
- È stato stupendo!
- Che tempo ha fatto?
- Ha fatto molto caldo, trentacinque gradi.

Page 74 Quiz

1 winter sports holiday; 2 Sorrento (all the others are islands); 3 vai; 4 andare, arrivare; 5 scendere (to come/go down, to get off a bus/train); 6 fa brutto tempo/che brutto tempo; 7 fa caldo is present, ha fatto caldo is past or perfect tense; 8 sono caduto/caduta.

Unit 8

Pages 76&77 Saying how you're feeling and describing symptoms

2 *Simona's not going into work because she's not well.*

3
- Simona, non stai bene?
- No, mi sento malissimo.
- Cos'hai?
- Non riesco a camminare. Ahia! Amelia, sto così male.
- Poverina! Ma cos'è successo? C'è stato un incidente?
- Un incidente? No. Ieri sono uscita con Lorenzo. Siamo andati in campagna e abbiamo camminato almeno cento chilometri.

- Simona, non esagerare!
- Beh almeno dieci chilometri. E sono caduta.
- Simona, ho molto da fare. Ciao.

4 Gianpietro, ciao. Simona non va al lavoro oggi. Non sta bene perché è andata in campagna ieri con Lorenzo ed è caduta. Baci.

5
- Stai meglio?
- No. Ahia! Mi fa male la schiena, mi fanno male le gambe e mi fa male il ginocchio.
- Se il ginocchio ti fa male, devi andare dal medico.

Her back, legs and knee hurt.

6
- Carla, sono io, Simona.
- Simona, ciao. Senti, non posso chiacchierare oggi. Luca non sta bene. Poverino, ha mal di gola, mal di testa, gli fanno male le spalle e ha la tosse. Ma tu, come stai?

Page 78 Following instructions

2
- Mi sono slogata il ginocchio.
- Aha. Mi faccia vedere. Cosa è successo?
- Sono caduta. Mi fa male.
- Riesce a piegarlo?
- Un po'. Con difficoltà.
- Hmm. Il ginocchio è un po' contuso – ma niente di grave. Prenda un antidolorifico, si riposi e faccia un po' di esercizio leggero.
- E basta?
- Sì sì. Fra due o tre giorni, tutto sarà a posto.

3
- Prenda due di queste capsule, con acqua, ogni quattro ore. Preferibilmente dopo i pasti. È importante non consumare alcol e non superare il dosaggio consigliato.

Take two capsules, with water, every four hours. Preferably after meals. It's important not to drink alcohol and not to exceed the recommended dose.

Page 79 Choosing alternative solutions

1 agopuntura, dieta bilanciata, armonia, medicina olistica, omeopatia, benessere interiore, massaggio, allenatore personale, stressato

Page 80 Put it all together

1 *a caviglia; b allenatore; c soccorso; d testa.*

2 *a 4 (5); b 3; c 2; d 1; e 7 (6); f 5; g 6.*

3 Ciao Daniele.
Mi dispiace ma non posso incontrarti stasera. Non sto bene, ho la febbre e mi fanno male le braccia e le gambe. Paola ha mal di gola e mal di testa. Tu, come stai? Sei andato al lavoro oggi? Hai visto Ugo?
Ciao

Page 81 Now you're talking!

1 • **Ciao! Stai bene?**
  ◆ No, non sto bene. Non sto bene per niente.
  • **Cos'hai?**
  ◆ Mi fa male la schiena e mi fa male il ginocchio.
  • **Poverina. Cos'è successo?**
  ◆ Cos'è successo? Ieri è successo!
  • **Ti sei divertita ieri?**
  ◆ Lorenzo, ieri abbiamo camminato venti chilometri e oggi non riesco ad alzarmi. Non riesco a ..
  • **Abbiamo camminato cinque chilometri. Beh ... ho molto da fare.**

2 • Come sta oggi?
  ◆ **Non sto bene.**
  • Mi dispiace. Cos'ha?
  ◆ **Ho mal di testa e mal di gola.**
  • Poverino.
  ◆ **E le spalle mi fanno male.**
  • Ha la febbre?
  ◆ **Sì, e ho la tosse e mal d'orecchio.**
  • Secondo me, ha l'influenza. Ha preso qualcosa?

  ◆ **No, ma voglio un antidolorifico.**
  • Io ho un prodotto omeopatico molto efficace. Aspetti un attimo.

Page 82 Quiz

1 Pronto Soccorso, 118; 2 sto male = I'm ill, sto meglio = I'm better; 3 mi fa male il piede, mi fanno male i piedi; 4 acupuncture is Chinese, shiatsu massage is Japanese; 5 ha mal di stomaco; 6 riesco; 7 può prendere (you can take; both the others tell you to take something); 8 I can't chat.

In più 4

Pages 83–86

1 *a* La settimana scorsa io **ho** scritto una lettera al giornale locale.
 b Mia figlia e mio genero **hanno** comprato una casa a Castelforte sei mesi fa.
 c Negli anni cinquanta io e mio marito **siamo** andati in Australia con i nostri figli.
 d L'anno scorso io **sono** tornata in Italia.
 e Mi **sono** sposata due anni dopo la fine della seconda guerra mondiale.
 f Quattro anni fa mio marito **è** morto.
 g Mi chiamo Antonia Ferrero; **sono** nata a Castelforte nel 1928.
 h Ieri il postino **ha** portato due risposte alla mia lettera.
 i Quindici giorni fa io **ho** deciso di cercare le mie vecchie compagne di classe.
 j Nel 1981 mia figlia **è** venuta a vivere a Roma.

2 *1 g; 2 e; 3 c; 4 j; 5 f; 6 d; 7 b; 8 i; 9 a; 10h.*
 Her name is Antonia Ferrero; she was born in Castelforte in 1928.
 Two years after the end of the Second World War she got married and in the 50s they went to Australia with their children.

In 1981 her daughter came to live in Rome.
Four years ago her husband died and last year she returned to Italy.
Six months ago her daughter and son-in-law bought a house in Castelforte. A fortnight ago she decided to try and find her old classmates and last week she wrote a letter to the local paper. Yesterday the postman brought two replies to her letter.

3 Antonia Ferrero abita a Castelforte, **una località termale** nel Lazio. **Le terme** sono le antiche Aquae Vescinae, frequentate dai Romani in epoca imperiale. **Il turismo termale** è diffuso in Italia, e molte persone vengono a Castelforte per **le proprietà terapeutiche** delle acque fredde, termali ed ipertermali che vanno dai 15° ai 69° C.

5 ● Signora, perché è venuta a Castelforte lei?
◆ Sono venuta per l'idroterapia, la ginnastica in acqua e il massaggio subacqueo.

● Signore, signora, perché siete venuti qui?
◆ Siamo venuti principalmente perché mia moglie soffre d'artrite.

● Posso chiedere perché siete venuti a Castelforte?
◆ Per motivi di salute. Io soffro di asma e vengo qui regolarmente perché trovo le acque benefiche.

◆ Le mie amiche, che sono venute l'anno scorso, sono andate pazze per i trattamenti estetici.

◆ Noi veniamo a Castelforte ogni anno per i trattamenti rilassanti.

● Perché è venuto a Castelforte?
◆ Da bambino, venivo in vacanza qui vicino con i miei genitori.
As a child, he used to come to the area on holiday with his parents.

6 *a* evidentemente; *b* in modo spettacolare, veramente; *c* bene, in modo intelligente, in modo professionale, sfortunatamente.

7 *a* *She can't leave her son (17) on his own – he fell while playing football and broke his leg.*
b *A friend who would like to come in her place.*

8 Gentile Signora Pelizza,
Sono John Kiel, un amico della signora McLeod. Lei ha disdetto la sua prenotazione perché suo figlio è caduto e si è rotto la gamba. Io vorrei venire a Villa Terracina al suo posto dal 21 al 28 aprile.
Distinti saluti

9 Ciao Elena
Come stai? Che cosa hai fatto a Pasqua? Io sono andato in Scozia. Ha fatto molto freddo ma mi sono alzato presto ogni mattina e ho passeggiato in montagna.
Vengo in Italia in aprile, dal 21 al 28. È da tanto tempo che non ci vediamo!
Baci John

Unit 9

Pages 88–89 Sending an invitation and replying

1 buongustaio; all'aperto; degustazione; Cantina Sociale; locale notturno.

2 *a* 1: Giulia, 2: Boris, 3: Sofia
b 8pm on Friday, on the terrace at the Casa Rustica.
c È invitata; sei invitato; ti piacerebbe.
d entro mercoledì

4 ● Ciao **Feixia**, sono Gio. Ti piacerebbere venire a cena alla Casa Rustica venerdì sera? È per festeggiare il compleanno di Claudia.
◆ **Che bell'idea. Volentieri.**

● **Pedro**, buongiorno. Sono Gio.

Questo venerdì è il compleanno di Claudia e abbiamo organizzato una cena per festeggiare. Avrà luogo venerdì sera, alle otto, sul terrazzo della Casa Rustica. Le piacerebbe venire?

♦ **Mi piacerebbe molto. Grazie mille.**

● Ciao **Nico**, sono Gio. Vi piacerebbe venire a una festa, tu e Leila? Facciamo una cena speciale venerdì sera ...

♦ Aiah Gio, **mi dispiace ma venerdì non possiamo. Che peccato!**

5 ♦ Sono Enrico. Ciao Gio – grazie per l'invito. Mi dispiace molto ma non posso venire alla cena perché venerdì **vado a Firenze**. Auguri a Claudia. Ciao.

Because he's going to Florence.

6 ● Ciao carissima. Hai ricevuto la mia mail?

♦ Sì, l'ho ricevuta.

● Allora? Hai voglia di venire alla cena?

♦ Boh ... **non so se posso.** Dov'è?

She doesn't know if she can come.

Pages 90&91 Saying what people are like and what they look like

2 ● Sofia viene alla cena?

♦ Non **so.**

● Non lo **sai?**

♦ Ha detto che non **sa se può** venire.

● Che **antipatica!**

3 ● Conosci Sofia?

♦ Non la conosco bene.

● Non viene alla cena – Pascal è molto **deluso.** È **vanitosa** quella ragazza.

♦ Secondo Pascal è **brava** e **gentile.**

● Secondo me, è davvero **antipatica.**

♦ Sono d'accordo con te. È **maleducata.**

● Povero Pascal. È così **simpatico** ... **educato** e **gentile.** Mi piace tanto.

♦ Che peccato che ha una cotta per Sofia.

P: deluso, simpatico, educato, gentile.
S: vanitosa, brava, gentile, antipatica, maleducata.
Gio agrees with Nadia: **Sono d'accordo con te.**

5 ● Ho ricevuto un messaggio da Gemma.

♦ Chi è Gemma?

● Frequenta il corso di fotografia.

♦ Com'è fisicamente? Ah, è mora e snella, vero?

● No, **è bionda, un po' in carne, alta circa un metro e sessantacinque.**

♦ No, non la conosco.

Gemma is blonde, a bit plump, 1m 65 tall.

6 ● Ma sì, la conosci. **Occhi marroni. Capelli lunghi e lisci.**

♦ Ah, Gemma! La ragazza con le gambe lunghe? Che sorride molto?

● Esatto!

Her hair is long and straight; her eyes are brown.

7 ● Ha risposto Boris?

♦ Chi è Boris? Il tizio grasso e basso con i baffi?

● No. **Non ha i baffi.** E **non è né grasso né magro.** Di solito, **si veste sportivo con jeans e scarpe da tennis. È alto quasi due metri e bello da morire.**

♦ Mmm.

No moustache, neither fat nor thin, he usually dresses casually in jeans and trainers; nearly two metres tall and drop-dead gorgeous.

Page 92 Put it all together

1 a Andiamo al ristorante.
  b Mangiamo all'aperto?
  c Esploriamo!
  d Parcheggiamo qui?
  e Andiamo a Roma domani.
  f Prenotiamo oggi e partiamo alle sette domani.

2 basso *short* alto *tall*; corto *short* lungo *long*; educato *polite* maleducato *rude*; magro *thin* grasso *fat*; biondo *blonde* moro *dark*; antipatico *unpleasant* simpatico/gentile *nice/kind*; snello *slim* in carne *plump*.

3 Cari amici
Siete **invitati** a una festa sabato 16 giugno. Per **festeggiare** il nostro anniversario di matrimonio, **abbiamo** organizzato una cena Da Luigi in via Tramontano poi **andiamo** al locale notturno in via Veneto.
Rispondere entro il 31 maggio per favore.
Saluti,
Rachele e Paolo.

4 Caro Salvatore, sei invitato a una festa venerdì, 12 ottobre. Per festeggiare il mio compleanno, ho organizzato una cena alla Trattoria Pescara alle otto di sera.
Rispondere entro il 30 settembre per favore.
Salut ...

5 ● Grazie. Che bell'idea! Mi piacerebbe molto venire.
● Mi dispiace. Che peccato! Non posso venire perché vado in vacanza.

Page 93 Now you're talking!

1 ● Sai che Leona non è andata al convegno?
◆ **Non conosco Leona.**
● Sì, la conosci. Lavora con Giorgio e Lavinia.
◆ **Com'è fisicamente? È alta?**
● Beh ... non è né alta né bassa. Un metro e sessanta, più o meno. Ha i capelli ricci, gli occhi marroni.
◆ **È bionda? Snella?**
● Bionda, sì. E abbastanza snella.
◆ **Sì, conosco Leona – è davvero simpatica.**

● Simpatica? Leona? Secondo me è poco simpatica.

2 ● Ciao. Tanto tempo che non ci vediamo! Senti, ti piacerebbe uscire per festeggiare il mio compleanno?
◆ **Che bell'idea! Mi piacerebbe molto.**
● Allora, martedì ho organizzato di andare al locale notturno in via Veneto.
◆ **Mi dispiace; martedì non posso perché vado a Milano.**
● Ah, che peccato! Ma senti, hai voglia di venire ad una festa da Marta? Avrà luogo il 3 dicembre.
◆ **Grazie mille, mi piacerebbe molto. Buon compleanno! E auguri a Marta.**

3 ● Com'è fisicamente, Leonardo?
◆ **È bello da morire: è moro, ha gli occhi neri, è alto un metro e ottanta e si veste sportivo.**

Page 94 Quiz
1 baffi; 2 sorry – mi dispiace; 3 una degustazione; 4 ultra nice, enormous, extraordinary; 5 ha luogo – the party takes place on Saturday; avrà luogo – the party will take place on Saturday; 6 che; 7 non so; 8 ho voglia.

Unit 10

Page 96 Following a recipe

2 ● Cuocere la pasta in modo corretto non è difficile se rispettiamo queste regole d'oro. Incominciamo con la pentola. Dev'essere grande – abbastanza grande per contenere almeno un litro d'acqua per ogni etto di pasta ... cioè, per ogni cento grammi di pasta. Mettiamo la pentola con l'acqua su un fuoco alto. Al punto di ebollizione, aggiungiamo poco a poco il sale: circa dieci grammi per ogni litro d'acqua. Poi versiamo la pasta nell'acqua e copriamo la pentola ... ma solo per qualche istante. Quando l'acqua riprende il punto di ebollizione, togliamo il coperchio. Manteniamo il fuoco alto perché l'acqua deve bollire vivacemente ... cioè, non sobbollire. Ogni tanto durante la cottura assaggiamo un pezzettino di pasta. Così. È cotta quando è al dente ... cioè, tenera all'esterno ma un po' dura all'interno.

◆ Quanti minuti?

● Dipende dal tipo di pasta. La pasta fresca è pronta molto prima della pasta secca – normalmente un minuto basta. Al punto di cottura, scoliamo rapidamente la pasta. È essenziale condire la pasta immediatamente in una scodella riscaldata. A tavola! La pasta è più buona se consumata prima possibile.

a La pentola dev'essere abbastanza grande per contenere almeno un litro d'acqua per ogni **cento** grammi di pasta.

b **Mettere** la pentola con l'acqua su un fuoco alto.

c Al punto di ebollizione, **aggiungere** poco a poco il sale: circa **dieci** grammi per ogni litro d'acqua.

d Versare la pasta nell'acqua e **coprire** per qualche istante.

e Quando l'acqua riprende il punto di ebollizione, **togliere** il coperchio e mantenere il fuoco alto.

f Durante la cottura **assaggiare** ogni tanto un pezzettino di pasta. È cotta quando è **al dente.** Per la pasta fresca, fatta in casa, **un** minuto basta normalmente.

g Al punto di cottura, **scolare** rapidamente la pasta e **condire** immediatamente in una scodella riscaldata.

h La pasta è più buona se consumata prima possibile.

3 *Golden rules for cooking pasta: large pan; one litre of water to every 100g of pasta; add salt when water is at boiling point; cover pan while bringing to the boil; when boiling, remove lid and cook pasta on high heat; taste regularly and don't overcook; drain, season and eat as soon as possible.*

Page 97 Choosing wine to complement a dish

2 *Antipasto:* bruschetta con porcini
Primo piatto: tagliatelle con salsa di cozze e broccoli
Pesce: alici fresche
Secondo piatto: agnello arrosto al rosmarino
Contorni: fagiolini e patate novelle
Formaggio: pecorino sardo
Frutta: frutta fresca
Dessert: torta al cioccolato e nocciole

3 ● Avete abbinato cibo e vino?
   ◆ Sì, ogni piatto è abbinato con un vino diverso. Come **aperitivo**, e da bere con gli antipasti, c'è un vino bianco spumante, leggero, non molto alcolico. **Un Prosecco.**
   ● Il Prosecco va servito fresco?
   ◆ Sì, fresco, a otto gradi.
   ● Da bere con il primo piatto?
   ◆ Il sugo per **le tagliatelle** è a base di cozze, e abbiamo **un Assisi** rosato. È giovane e delicato. Poi, con **il pesce** serviamo **un Torgiano** bianco secco.
   ● Questi vini vengono serviti freschi o a temperatura ambiente?
   ◆ Tutti e due vengono serviti freschi.
   ● E per il secondo piatto?
   ◆ Con **l'agnello** abbiamo un vino rosso corposo, **un Montepulciano d'Abruzzo** del 2005. Un rosso anche con **il formaggio** – un

eccellente pecorino sardo – che abbiamo abbinato con **un Chianti Classico.**

● Com'è il Chianti?

◆ Intenso e robusto. Poi, **il dessert** è frutta fresca e torta al cioccolato che serviremo con un vino rosso liquoroso e dolce – **un Marsala.**

● Brava! Allora ... a tavola. Buon appetito.

Aperitivo: Prosecco; *primo piatto:* Assisi; *pesce:* Torgiano; *secondo piatto:* Montepulciano d'Abruzzo; *formaggio:* Chianti Classico; *dessert:* Marsala.

4 *Prosecco:* bianco, leggero, spumante; *Assisi:* rosato, giovane, delicato; *Torgiano:* bianco, secco; *Montepulciano d'Abruzzo:* rosso, corposo; *Chianti Classico:* rosso, intenso, robusto; *Marsala:* rosso, liquoroso, dolce.

Page 98 Commenting on a meal

2 ● Andrea, vuole assaggiare questo vino bianco?

◆ Mm ... secco, leggero, delicato ... ha un sapore elegante.

● È molto robusto questo vino rosso.

◆ Sì, è davvero corposo.

● Le è piaciuto l'agnello arrosto?

◆ Mi è piaciuto moltissimo – cotto a perfezione.

● Hai assaggiato il pecorino?

◆ È un po' troppo forte per me come formaggio, troppo salato.

● Troppo forte – assolutamente no! È squisito, è il mio formaggio preferito.

● Cosa pensi della torta?

◆ Perfetta! Non troppo dolce. Secondo me, contiene del rum.

a 4; b 5; c 1; d 2; e 3.

3 ● Cosa pensi della torta?

◆ Perfetta! Non troppo dolce. Secondo me, contiene del rum.

Mi ricorda la torta che mia zia preparava per il compleanno di mio zio. Ogni anno. La serviva con panna e Prosecco.

Giulia's aunt used to make one like it, every year for her uncle's birthday.

Page 99 Expressing your appreciation

2 ● Allora, complimenti agli chef, alla classe del 2007. È stata una splendida cena. Splendida. È andata a meraviglia; il primo piatto in particolare è stato eccellente – un capolavoro.

◆ Un brindisi agli chef.

● Agli chef!

◆ Ora, mi fa molto piacere augurare un buon compleanno a mia moglie. Claudia, da parte di tutti, auguri. Buon compleanno!

● Buon compleanno!

splendida (splendid); first course (tagliatelle); the chefs/the class of 2007; his wife Claudia's.

3 *Three things: cooking an Italian meal; matching food and wine; speaking Italian better.*

Page 100 Put it all together

1 *a 6; b 7; c 10; d 8; e 2; f 9; g 1; h 3; i 5; j 4.*

2 *Correct order: g, c, d, a, h, f, b, e.*

3 comincio *Present* I start/I'm starting; dormirò *Future* I will sleep; telefonerò *Future* I will phone; andavo *Imperfect* I was going/I used to go; abito *Present* I live/I'm living; lavoravo *Imperfect* I was working/I used to work; giocavo *Imperfect* I was playing/I used to play; finirò *Future* I will finish; avevo *Imperfect* I used to have; penso *Present* I think/I'm thinking.

1   • Ti piace il risotto?
     ◆ **È eccellente, cotto a perfezione.**
     • Devi assaggiare questo pecorino. È così buono.
     ◆ **Sì, è buonissimo. Hai assaggiato il gorgonzola?**
     • Il gorgonzola – il mio formaggio preferito! Hm, ma questo è ancora piuttosto giovane … E il vino? Cosa ne pensi?
     ◆ **È splendido, così robusto e corposo. Mi piace.**
     • Sono buoni i nostri vini italiani, vero?
     ◆ **Mi è piaciuto molto l'aperitivo, il Prosecco.**

2   • Che bella torta!
     ◆ **L' ho fatta io, da una ricetta di mia nonna. Contiene mandorle. Lei non è allergico alle noci?**
     • No, non sono allergico alle noci.
     ◆ Cosa ne pensa?
     • Mi piace molto; mi ricorda una ricetta francese. Complimenti allo chef!
     ◆ Domani le do la ricetta.
     • Grazie mille, Fabrizio. Mi sono divertito tanto. Arrivederci.

1 un litro d'acqua e 10 grammi di sale; 2 low heat; 3 assaggiare; 4 coperchio – cover; 5 cioè; 6 lavoravano; 7 va; 8 brindisi.

al dente: tenera all'esterno ma un po' dura all'interno
sobbollire: cuocere a fuoco basso/non bollire vivacemente
tagliatelle: una specie di pasta
prosecco: un vino frizzante italiano
amabile: né dolce né secco
splendido: eccellente/meraviglioso
condire: aggiungere sale, pepe, salsa

In più 5

Pages 103–106

1 *a vero; b falso; c vero; d falso; e falso; f vero; g vero; h vero.*

2 *Paese dove si trova la proprietà:* Inghilterra, Gran Bretagna.
Tipo di proprietà: Casa indipendente di nuova costruzione
Numero di camere da letto: 4
Numero di bagni: 3

Caratteristiche della proprietà:
giardino ✓   *box/parcheggio* ✓
terrazzo ✓   *vista panoramica* ✓
balcone ✗   *piscina privata* ✗
aria condizionata ✗
riscaldamento centrale ✓

Comfort in dotazione:
cucina moderna ✓   *lavastoviglie* ?
televisione ?   *accesso internet* ?
ascensore ✗   *caminetto* ✓
Prossimità a:
negozi ✓   *ristoranti* ?
spiaggia ?   *parco giochi* ✓
piscina pubblica ?   *trasporti pubblici* ✓
palestra ?   *campo da golf* ✓

3   • Benvenuti in Italia. Io sono Loredana.
     ◆ **Piacere. Io sono Rob. Mia moglie non è qui, è andata in città.**
     • Sua moglie, come si chiama?
     ◆ **Si chiama Samira.**
     • Le piace l'Umbria?
     ◆ **Mi piace molto – è così bella e interessante.**
     • È il vostro primo soggiorno in Italia?
     ◆ **Siamo venuti a Roma due anni fa. L'anno scorso siamo andati in Francia – ma preferiamo l'Italia. Io vado pazzo per l'Italia; studio l'italiano da due anni.**
     • Allora, che cosa avete visto nella regione?
     ◆ **Lunedì, da solo, sono andato a**

Perugia dove ho visto il Palazzo dei Priori. Mi è piaciuto molto.

- Che tempo ha fatto?
- **Ha fatto caldo.**
- A che ora è andato?
- **Sono partito alle otto di mattina.**
- E cos'avete fatto martedì?
- **Siamo andati ad Arezzo dove abbiamo visitato il museo**
- Avete visto lo splendido Duomo?
- **Sì, abbiamo visto il Duomo ma, sfortunatamente, non abbiamo fotografie perché abbiamo perso la macchina fotografica.**
- Che peccato! Avete fatto una denuncia?
- **Sì, siamo andati alla questura a Perugia.**
- Mah ... un altro bicchiere di vino, Rob?
- **No, grazie. Ci siamo divertiti molto ma dobbiamo andare. Grazie mille.**
- Prego. All'anno prossimo!

4 Carissima Mariella

Siamo arrivati in Italia, stiamo in una grande casa indipendente vicino a Perugia. C'è un supermercato vicino e abbiamo trovato una piccola trattoria.

Ha fatto molto caldo domenica. Ci siamo alzati presto e siamo andati a Foligno.

Lunedì Rob è andato a Perugia dove ha visto il Palazzo dei Priori. Io ho comprato un sacco di cose al mercato!

C'è una splendida vista qui. Comunque non abbiamo fotografie perché martedì pomeriggio Rob ha smarrito la macchina fotografica. Abbiamo fatto una denuncia alla questura e compilato il modulo. Poi abbiamo sbagliato strada e siamo tornati a casa dopo mezzanotte!

È stato meraviglioso ... e torneremo in Italia l'anno prossimo.

Bacioni, Samira

pronunciation and spelling

1 **Italian vowels** are pure and consistent sounds.

a	pasta or banana, Marsala
e/è	espresso, caffè
e/é	crema
i	panini
o	broccoli or ravioli, Barolo
u	cappuccino, tiramisù

2 **Consonants** other than the following sound very similar in Italian and English. **H** is never sounded.

	English sound	Examples
ce, ci	ch	dolcelatte, spinaci
ch	k	radicchio, Chianti
c + other letters	k	caffè, cornetto
ge, gi	j	gelato, formaggio
gn	ni	gnocchi
gli	lli	tagliatelle
g + other letters	g	spaghetti, gorgonzola
r	rolled	risotto, birra
sce/sci	sh	prosciutto
sch	sk	bruschetta
sc + other letters	sk	mascarpone, Lambrusco
z	dz or tz	zucchini, pizza

3 The letters j, k, w, x and y are not part of the Italian alphabet, but are used to spell foreign words.

4 Double consonants are pronounced with double the sound: **nn** in panna and penne sounds like unnecessary in English.

5 As a general rule, words are stressed on the last syllable but one, but there are many exceptions. A few words have a written accent to indicate stress, but most can only be learned by listening.

6 **Accents**

- indicate a final stressed vowel: città, perché, così, però, più;
- differentiate between two words which otherwise look and sound the same: **da** *from*, **dà** *gives*.

numbers and dates

0 zero	15 quindici	30 trenta
1 uno	16 sedici	40 quaranta
2 due	17 diciassette	50 cinquanta
3 tre	18 diciotto	60 sessanta
4 quattro	19 diciannove	70 settanta
5 cinque	20 venti	80 ottanta
6 sei	21 ventuno	90 novanta
7 sette	22 ventidue	100 cento
8 otto	23 ventitré	200 duecento
9 nove	24 ventiquattro	1.000 mille
10 dieci	25 venticinque	2.000 duemila
11 undici	26 ventisei	1.000.000 un milione
12 dodici	27 ventisette	2.000.000 due milioni
13 tredici	28 ventotto	
14 quattordici	29 ventinove	

- 31 to 99 follow the same pattern as 21 to 29: **trentuno, trentadue, trentatré,** etc.

1st primo	6th sesto
2nd secondo	7th settimo
3rd terzo	8th ottavo
4th quarto	9th nono
5th quinto	10th decimo

- For ordinal numbers after 10th, **-esimo** is added to the number minus its final vowel: 11th **undicesimo**, 20th **ventesimo**, 100th **centesimo**.

lunedì (m) *Monday*	giovedì (m) *Thursday*
martedì (m) *Tuesday*	venerdì (m) *Friday*
mercoledì (m) *Wednesday*	sabato (m) *Saturday*
	domenica (f) *Sunday*

gennaio *January*	**luglio** *July*
febbraio *February*	**agosto** *August*
marzo *March*	**settembre** *September*
aprile *April*	**ottobre** *October*
maggio *May*	**novembre** *November*
giugno *June*	**dicembre** *December*

- Dates are written **il 3 agosto** and said **il tre agosto**.

grammar

This section uses the key grammatical terms defined on page 6.

G1 **Nouns** are all either masculine (m) or feminine (f).

Singular nouns ending in	In the **plural**
-o : nearly always m	**-o** ▸ **-i**
-a : generally f	**-a** ▸ **-e**
-e : some m, some f	**-e** ▸ **-i**

But:
- **-ista** nouns can be m or f: **il/la giornalista**;
- most **-ma** nouns are m: **il problema, il clima**;
- foreign nouns and nouns ending in an accented vowel don't change in the plural: **gli chef, le specialità**;
- most nouns ending in **-ga/-go/-ca/-co** add **h** in the plural: **amica ▸ amiche, luogo ▸ luoghi**. But when **-co** follows a vowel, **h** is not normally added: **amico ▸ amici**.

G2 **Articles** have masculine and feminine forms.

	a/an	*the* (singular)	*the* (plural)	before …
m	**un giorno**	**il giorno**	**i giorni**	consonant
	uno sconto	**lo sconto**	**gli sconti**	z, s +consonant
	un anno	**l'anno**	**gli anni**	vowel
f	**una lista**	**la lista**	**le liste**	consonant
	un'idea	**l'idea**	**le idee**	vowel

G3 Some **prepositions** correspond to more than one English usage.

a	*at*	a casa, a mezzogiorno
	in	abito a Londra
	to	vado a Roma
da	*from*	a 2 km da Roma
	since/for	lavoro qui da aprile/da 5 anni
	for (purpose)	occhiali da sole, campo da golf
di	*of*	una bottiglia di vino, una borsa di pelle
	than	questa è più cara di quella
in	*in*	abito in Inghilterra
	to	vado in Inghilterra
	by	vado in aereo/in macchina
per	*for*	una lettera per me
	in order to	per comunicare con Anna

G4 Prepositions **a**, **da**, **di**, **in** and **su** *on* combine with the definite article.

	il	lo	l'	la	i	gli	le
a	al	allo	all'	alla	ai	agli	alle
da	dal	dallo	dall'	dalla	dai	dagli	dalle
di	del*	dello*	dell'*	della*	dei*	degli*	delle*
in	nel	nello	nell'	nella	nei	negli	nelle
su	sul	sullo	sull'	sulla	sui	sugli	sulle

*these words can also mean *some*.

G5 **Adjectives** agree with what they describe.

Adjectives ending in -**o** have four forms:

	singular	plural
m	vino italiano	vini italiani
f	birra italiana	birre italiane

Adjectives ending in -**e** have only two forms:

	singular	plural
m	vino francese	vini francesi
f	birra francese	birre francesi

G6 In the plural, adjectives:

- describing a combination of m and f nouns use the m form:
  Il vino e la torta sono italiani.
- ending in -**co** after a consonant, and -**go**, add **h**: bianco ▸ bianchi, bianche; largo ▸ larghi, larghe
- ending in -**co** after a vowel add **h** only in the feminine:
  storico ▸ i centri storici, le città storiche

G7 **Position:** when adjectives and nouns are next to each other:

- adjectives generally go after the noun:
  una vista magnifica, il vino bianco
- but common adjectives like **bello/brutto**, **buono/cattivo**, **grande/piccolo**, **breve/lungo**, often (see note 8) go before the noun:
  una breve storia, un piccolo aperitivo
- **primo, secondo, terzo** etc. also go before the noun:
  la seconda strada
- adjectives sometimes change their usual position for emphasis:
  una magnifica vista, un aperitivo piccolo

G8 When **buono, grande** and **bello** go before a noun:

- **buono/a** and **grande** often shorten to **buon** and **gran**:
  un buon vino, una buon'idea, un gran piacere, la Gran Bretagna
- **bello** has endings similar to the definite article, listed on page 65:
  un bel sole, un bell'albergo
  However, it is regular when on its own or after a noun:
  bello, bella, belli, belle

G9 Possessives: the definite article is used with possessive adjectives, which agree with the gender of what's owned, not the owner. *My car* is always **la mia macchina**.

my	il mio	la mia	i miei	le mie
your **tu**	il tuo	la tua	i tuoi	le tue
your **lei**, *his/her*	il suo	la sua	i suoi	le sue
our	il nostro	la nostra	i nostri	le nostre
your **voi**	il vostro	la vostra	i vostri	le vostre
their	il loro	la loro	i loro	le loro

When talking about just one member of the family, the definite article is used only with **loro**:
mia madre, suo fratello, vostro padre but **la loro nonna**.

G10 **Questo** *this* and **quello** *that*:

- always go before the noun, where **quello** has endings similar to the definite article, listed in full on page 65:
  questa casa, quel vestito, quei vestiti
- mean *this one/that one* or *these/those* without a noun:
  Mi piace questa; Non mi piacciono quelle.
- often have **qui** *here* and **lì** *there* added in comparisons:
  Questa qui o quella lì?

G11 Adverbs can be formed by:

- adding -**mente** to a f sing adjective:
  chiaro ▸ chiaramente, semplice ▸ semplicemente
- using **in modo** + m adjective:
  in modo elegante

Other common adverbs include **molto** *very*, **un po'** *a bit*, **troppo** *too*, **così** *so*, **piuttosto** *rather*.
The ending of an adverb never changes:
una giacca *molto* **cara**
Queste scarpe sono *troppo* **strette.**

G12   **Comparison:** adjectives and adverbs are compared with **più** *more* and **meno** *less*:

più elegante *more stylish*, **più stretto** *tighter*,
meno caro *less expensive*, **meno rapidamente** *less quickly*;
- *Than* is **di** (or **del, della**, etc. when followed by *the*)
  La giacca è più cara del vestito. *The jacket is dearer than the dress.*
- *The* + **più/meno** means *the most/least*:
  la più elegante *the most stylish*, **il meno caro** *the least expensive*.

G13   There are **three groups of verbs**, ending in -**are**, -**ere**, -**ire** in the infinitive (*to do*). The -**are**, -**ere**, -**ire** ending changes in a predictable, regular way according to:

- subject: who/what is carrying out the action of the verb,
- tense: when it takes place.

G14   **Subject pronouns:** since the ending of the verb is enough to indicate who/what is doing something, the subject pronouns **io** *I*, **tu/lei** *you*, **lui/lei** *he/she*, **noi** *we*, **voi** *you* and **loro** *they* are used only for emphasis, contrast or clarification.

There are three words for *you*, each using a different verb ending:
tu: someone you call by their first name;
lei: (occasionally written **Lei**) someone you don't know well, someone older;
voi: more than one person.

G15   **Present tense**

- The equivalent of *do, am/is/are doing*.
- With **da**, it translates as *have been doing*: **Lavoro qui da aprile/da un anno.** *I've been working here since April/for a year.*
- The **noi** form can mean *we do, we're doing* or *Let's do*.
- In this tense only, -**ire** verbs fall into two sub-groups. There's no way of predicting whether an -**ire** verb adds -**isc** but the most common verbs following this pattern are **capire, finire, preferire, spedire, costruire, pulire** and **gestire**.

	abit**are**	vend**ere**	part**ire**	cap**ire**
io	abit**o**	vend**o**	part**o**	cap**isco**
tu	abit**i**	vend**i**	part**i**	cap**isci**
lei, lui/lei	abit**a**	vend**e**	part**e**	cap**isce**
noi	abit**iamo**	vend**iamo**	part**iamo**	cap**iamo**
voi	abit**ate**	vend**ete**	part**ite**	cap**ite**
loro	abit**ano**	vend**ono**	part**ono**	cap**iscono**

Verbs ending in -**care**/-**gare** preserve their sound with **tu** and **noi** by adding -**h**-:

cercare ▸ cerco *but* cerchi, cerchiamo
spiegare ▸ spiego *but* spieghi, spieghiamo.

G16 **Irregular verbs:** not all verbs follow the regular patterns. The following common verbs are irregular in the present tense.

andare	to go	vado, vai, va, andiamo, andate, vanno
avere	to have[1]	ho, hai, ha, abbiamo, avete, hanno
dare	to give	do, dai, dà, diamo, date, danno
dire	to say	dico, dici, dice, diciamo, dite, dicono
dovere	to have to	devo, devi, deve, dobbiamo, dovete, devono
essere	to be	sono, sei, è, siamo, siete, sono
fare	to do, make[1]	faccio, fai, fa, facciamo, fate, fanno
potere	to be able to	posso, puoi, può, possiamo, potete, possono
sapere	to know	so, sai, sa, sappiamo, sapete, sanno
stare	to be[2]	sto, stai, sta, stiamo, state, stanno
tenere	to hold	tengo, tieni, tiene, teniamo, tenete, tengono
uscire	to go out	esco, esci, esce, usciamo, uscite, escono
venire	to come	vengo, vieni, viene, veniamo, venite, vengono
volere	to want	voglio, vuoi, vuole, vogliamo, volete, vogliono

[1] see note 18   [2] see note 17

G17 **Present continuous:** in order to emphasise that something is taking place right at the moment, the present tense of **stare** can be used with the gerund, formed by replacing -**are** with -**ando**, -**ere** and -**ire** with -**endo**: **sto guardando** *I'm browsing;* **stiamo mangiando** *we're (in the process of) eating.*

G18 In many phrases, **avere** and **fare** (often shortened to **aver'** and **far'**) are not translated into English as *have* and *do/make*:

avere bisogno di *to need*
avere paura *to be afraid*
avere voglia di *to feel like*
avere fame *to be hungry*
avere caldo *to be hot*
avere ragione *to be right*

avere luogo *to take place*
avere sonno *to feel sleepy*
avere fretta *to be in a hurry*
avere sete *to be thirsty*
avere freddo *to be cold*
avere torto *to be wrong*

fare attenzione *to pay attention*
fare la spesa *to go food shopping*
fare una pausa *to take a break*
fare una domanda *to ask a question*

fare una foto *to take a photo*
fare colazione *to have breakfast*
fare il trekking *to go rambling*
fare una passeggiata *to go for a walk*

G19 ## Future tense

- The equivalent of *will/shall do.*
- The endings all include a distinctive -**r**- sound.

	abit**are**	vend**ere**	part**ire**
io	abit**erò**	vend**erò**	part**irò**
tu	abit**erai**	vend**erai**	part**irai**
lei, lei/lui	abit**erà**	vend**erà**	part**irà**
noi	abit**eremo**	vend**eremo**	part**iremo**
voi	abit**erete**	vend**erete**	part**irete**
loro	abit**eranno**	vend**eranno**	part**iranno**

- **essere**: sarò, sarai, sarà, saremo, sarete, saranno
- Verbs ending in -**care**/-**gare** add -**h**- before the endings: cercherò, spiegheranno.
- **Andare**, **avere**, **dovere**, **potere** and **vedere** drop the penultimate vowel: **andrò, andrai, andrà, andremo**, etc.
- **Bere**, **rimanere**, **venire** and **volere** have a double **r**: **berrò, berrai, berrà, berremo, berrete, berranno.**
- **Dare**, **fare** and **stare** retain the **a** of their -**are** infinitive ending, unlike regular -**are** verbs (which change **a** to **e**): **darò, darai, darà, daremo, darete, daranno.**

G20 ## Imperfect tense

- The equivalent of *was/were doing, used to do.*
- The endings all include a distinctive -**v**- sound.

	abit**are**	vend**ere**	part**ire**
io	abit**avo**	vend**evo**	part**ivo**
tu	abit**avi**	vend**evi**	part**ivi**
lei, lei/lui	abit**ava**	vend**eva**	part**iva**
noi	abit**avamo**	vend**evamo**	part**ivamo**
voi	abit**avate**	vend**evate**	part**ivate**
loro	abit**avano**	vend**evano**	part**ivano**

- **essere**: ero, eri, era, eravamo, eravate, erano

G21   **Perfect tense**

- The equivalent of *did, have done.*
- Most verbs form the perfect tense with the present tense of **avere** + the past participle of the main verb (see note 22).
- A few verbs, mainly relating to movement, use the present tense of **essere** instead of **avere**. Reflexive verbs (see note 26) also use **essere**.

G22   **Past participles** (pp) are formed by changing:

-are to **-ato**:	**abitare ▸ abitato**
-ere to **-uto**:	**vendere ▸ venduto, avere ▸ avuto**
-ire to **-ito**:	**partire ▸ partito**

The past participles of several common verbs are irregular, e.g.:

aprire *to open* (pp **aperto**)
bere *to drink* (pp **bevuto**)
chiedere *to ask* (pp **chiesto**)
chiudere *to close* (pp **chiuso**)
dire *to say* (pp **detto**)
essere *to be* (pp **stato**)
fare *to do/make* (pp **fatto**)
leggere *to read* (pp **letto**)

mettere *to put* (pp **messo**)
offrire *to offer* (pp **offerto**)
perdere *to lose* (pp **perso**)
prendere *to take* (pp **preso**)
rispondere *to answer* (pp **risposto**)
scegliere *to choose* (pp **scelto**)
scrivere *to write* (pp **scritto**)
vedere *to see* (pp **visto**)

G23   **Perfect tense with avere**

io	ho	
tu	hai	
lei, lui/lei	ha	**capito**
noi	abbiamo	
voi	avete	
loro	hanno	

G24   **Perfect tense with essere**

- The ending of the past participle agrees with the subject.
- All reflexive verbs use **essere** (see note 26).

		m	f
io	sono	andato	andata
tu	sei		
lei, lui/lei	è		
noi	siamo	andati	andate
voi	siete		
loro	sono		

The following are the most common **essere** verbs. The past participle is included only where it is irregular.

andare to go
arrivare to arrive
cadere to fall
diventare to become
entrare to enter
essere to be (pp **stato**)
morire to die (pp **morto**)
nascere to be born (pp **nato**)
partire to leave/depart
restare to stay/remain

rimanere to remain (pp **rimasto**)
(ri)tornare to return
riuscire to succeed in
salire to go up/get into
scendere to go down/get off
(pp **sceso**)
stare to be
succedere to happen (pp **successo**)
uscire to go out
venire to come (pp **venuto**)

G25 Pluperfect tense

- The equivalent of *had done*.
- Formed by putting a past participle after the imperfect of **avere** (regular) and **essere** (irregular):
  avevo mangiato *I had eaten*; **ero arrivato** *I had arrived*

G26 Reflexive verbs: the infinitive of reflexive verbs ends in -si: **chiamarsi** *to be called*, **alzarsi** *to get up*, **sposarsi** *to get married*.

These verbs follow exactly the same pattern of endings as regular **-are**, **-ere**, **-ire** verbs, but also include **mi**, **ti**, **si**, **ci** or **vi** before the verb according to who/what is involved.

	present	perfect
io	**mi** alz**o**	**mi sono** alz**ato/a**
tu	**ti** alz**i**	**ti sei** alz**ato/a**
lei, lui/lei	**si** alz**a**	**si è** alz**ato/a**
noi	**ci** alz**iamo**	**ci siamo** alz**ati/e**
voi	**vi** alz**ate**	**vi siete** alz**ati/e**
loro	**si** alz**ano**	**si sono** alz**ati/e**

G27 Negatives: to make a negative statement, **non** goes before the verb. With reflexive verbs, it goes before **mi**, **ti**, **si**, etc.

Non lavoro questa settimana e non mi alzo presto.

Non stays in the same sentence as words like **niente** *nothing*, **nessuno** *nobody*, **mai** *never*, **né ... né** *neither... nor*:
Non mangio mai. *I never eat.*
Non mangio né carne né pesce. *I eat neither meat nor fish.*
Non ho mangiato niente. *I ate nothing, I didn't eat anything.*

G28   **Imperatives** can be used to give directions or instructions.

	tu	lei	voi
scusare	scusa	scusi	scusate
riposarsi	riposati	si riposi	riposatevi
prendere	prendi	prenda	prendete
dormire	dormi	dorma	dormite
capire	capisci	capisca	capite

You'll see the **infinitive** used instead of the imperative:
- for official instructions: **aprire con cautela** *open with caution*;
- to tell someone (**tu**) not to do something: **non esagerare!**
- very often in recipes: **mescolare bene**.

Dovere *to have to* + infinitive is another alternative: **deve girare a destra**.

G29   **Questions** can be formed with a question word:

Cosa/Che? *What?*	**Chi?** *Who/Whom?* (see note 30)
Come? *How?*	**Dove?** *Where?*
Perché? *Why?*	**Quando?** *When?*
Quale/i? *Which?*	**Quanto/a?** *How much?*
Quanti/e? *How many?*	

They can also be formed simply by raising the voice at the end of a statement so that it sounds like a question.

They often have **vero?** added to them, the equivalent of all English phrases like *isn't it?, aren't we? don't they? didn't he?*.

G30   **Chi and che:** Although **chi** is *who* in a question, **che** translates *who, whom, which* and *that* in sentences like the following:

L'idraulico che lavora qui. *The plumber who works here.*
Le ragazze che ho visto. *The girls (whom) I saw.*
La casa che ho comprato. *The house that I bought.*

G31   **Ne** can mean *of it/them* or *some/any* and, more often than not, is not translated into English. When **ci** is before **ne**, it changes to **ce**; **c'è** becomes **ce n'è**, and **ci sono** becomes **ce ne sono**: **ce n'è uno, ce ne sono tre**.

G32   **Direct and indirect object pronouns:** when the object of a verb is a pronoun, it can be a direct object (e.g. *me, him, us*) or indirect (e.g. *to me, to him, to us*). In Italian these are differentiated in the 3rd person only.

direct		indirect	
mi	*me*	**mi**	*to me*
ti	*you*	**ti**	*to you*
lo	*him/it*	**gli**	*to him*
la	*her/it/you* (**lei**)	**le**	*to her/you* (**lei**)
ci	*us*	**ci**	*to us*
vi	*you*	**vi**	*to you*
li	*them* (m)	**gli/loro**	*to them*
le	*them* (f)		

Note: **lo/la** are the only object pronouns to shorten to **l'**:
l'apprezzo *I appreciate it,* **Maria l'ha visto** *Maria saw him.*

G33 **Position:** both sets normally go in front of the verb:

La lavo a mano. *I wash it (**la maglia**) by hand.*
Gianni mi ha telefonato. *Gianno phoned (to) me.*
But with **dovere**, **potere** and **volere**, they can either go at the end of the verb in the infinitive:
Vorrei provarlo, **Posso cambiarli?**
or before the two verbs:
Lo vorrei provare, **Li posso cambiare?**

G34 **Agreement:** in the past tenses the past participle agrees with the direct object pronouns **la**, **lo**, **li**, **le**:

Maria l'ha vista *Maria saw her,* **Le ho comprate ieri** (referring to **le scarpe**).

G35 **Indirect object pronouns** are needed with verbs like **piacere**, **interessare** and **fare male** because their literal meaning is *to be pleasing to, to be of interest to* and *to do harm to*:

Le piace questo? *Do you (**lei**) like this?* **Le fa male il piede** *Her foot hurts;* **Gli interessa il calcio?** *Is he interested in football?*

Indirect object pronouns are also needed with verbs like **telefonare** or **offrire**, where *to* is understood but not expressed in English:
gli ho telefonato *I phoned (to) him;* **le abbiamo offerto un caffè** *we offered (to) her a coffee.*

G36 After a preposition, the emphatic pronouns **me**, **te**, **lui**, **lei**, **noi**, **voi**, **loro** are used: **da me**, **secondo lui**, **per noi**, **con loro**.

Italian–English glossary

This glossary contains the words found in this book, with their meanings in the contexts used here. Most verbs are given only in the infinitive, but parts of some irregular Italian verbs are also included. Abbreviations: (m) masculine, (f) feminine, (sing) singular, (pl) plural, (adj) adjective, (adv) adverb. Unless otherwise indicated, nouns ending in -o are masculine, and those ending in -a and -à are feminine. Adjectives are in the masculine singular form.

A

a at, to
abbastanza enough
abbiamo we have
abbinare to match
abbraccio hug
abitare to live
accanto next to
accesso access
accessorio accessory
accordo agreement:
    d'accordo agreed, OK
aceto vinegar
acqua water
acquazzone (m) shower
adatto suitable
addetto/a stampa press officer
adesso now
aerobico aerobic
aeroporto airport
affare (m) deal, bargain
affettuoso affectionate
affitto rent
    in affitto to rent
agente di polizia (m/f) police officer
agente immobiliare (m/f) estate agent
agenzia immobiliare estate agent's
aggiungere to add
agli at/to the (m pl)
agnello lamb
agopuntura acupuncture
agricolo agricultural
agriturismo rural tourism
ai at/to the (m pl)
aiutare to help
aiuto help
albero tree
alcol (m) alcohol
alcolico alcoholic

alice (f) anchovy
alimentazione (f) nutrition
allegro cheerful
allenarsi to train
allenatore (m) trainer
allergico allergic
alloggio accommodation
allora well
almeno at least
altezza height
alto tall
altro other
alzarsi to get up
amabile medium-sweet (wine)
americano American
amico/a friend
ammirare to admire
ampio large, ample
analista (m/f) analyst
anche also, even
ancora still, again
andare to go
angolo corner
anniversario anniversary
anno year
    gli anni cinquanta the 1950s
antichità antiquity
antico ancient, antique
antidolorifico painkiller
antipasto hors d'œuvres
antipatico unpleasant
antiquato antiquated
aperitivo aperitif
aperto open
    all'aperto open-air
apertura opening
appartamento apartment
appoggiare to lean, to put down
apprezzare to appreciate

appuntamento appointment
aprire to open
Arabia Saudita Saudi Arabia
archeologico archeological
architetto architect
argento silver
armadio wardrobe
armonia harmony
arredato furnished, equipped
arrivare to arrive
arrivederci goodbye
arrosto roasted
arte (f) art
articolo article
artistico artistic
artrite (f) arthritis
ascensore (m) lift
asciugabiancheria dryer
asma asthma
assaggiare to taste
assicurazione (f) insurance
assolutamente absolutely
assumere to assume
astrologia astrology
atrio entrance hall
attimo moment
attore/attrice (m/f) actor
attraversare to cross
attrezzato equipped
attualmente currently
augurare to wish
augurio wish
auto (f) car
autobus (m) bus
avere to have
avventura adventure
avvocato lawyer
Azzorre (fpl) Azores
azzurro blue

B

bacio kiss
　bacioni (m pl) big kisses
baffi (m pl) moustache
bagno bath, bathroom
　bagno di servizio utility
　bathroom
balcone (m) balcony
bambino baby, small child
banca bank
banchiere (m) banker
bancomat (m) cashpoint
banconota (f) banknote
basso short
bastare to be enough
beati voi! lucky you!
beh well
bei (m pl) beautiful
Belgio Belgium
bellino cute
bello lovely, beautiful
bene fine, well
benefico beneficial
benessere (m) well-being
bianco white
bicchiere (m) drinking glass
bici, bicicletta bike, bicycle
bifamiliare semi-detached
biglietto ticket
　biglietto di auguri
　greetings card
bilanciato balanced
bilocale two-roomed
binocolo (m sing)
binoculars
biodiversità biodiversity
biondo blonde
bip (m) beep
birra beer
bisnonna great-
grandmother
bisnonno great-
grandfather
bisogna you need to
bisogno need
　avere bisogno di to
　need
blu navy blue
bocca mouth
bollettino bulletin
bollire to boil
borsetta handbag
borsone (m) holdall

box (m) garage
braccio (m) arm
　le braccia (f pl) arms
Brasile (m) Brazil
bravo good
breve brief, short
brindisi (m) toast
bruno brown
brutto ugly, nasty
buongustaio gourmet
buono good
burro butter
bussola compass

C

c'è there is/are
cachemire (m) cashmere
cadere to fall
caffè (m) coffee
calcio football
caldo hot
calendario calendar
cambiamento change
cambiare to change
camera (bed)room
cameriera waitress
cameriere (m) waiter
camicia shirt
camino, caminetto
fireplace
camminare to walk
campagna the countryside
campeggio campsite
campionati (m pl)
championships
campo da golf golf course
canarino canary
cantante (m/f) singer
cantina cellar, vineyard
capelli (m pl) hair
capiente capacious
capire to understand
capo chief, head
capolavoro masterpiece
capoluogo principal town
cappello hat
cappuccio hood
capsula capsule
Carabinieri Military Police
Caraibi (m pl) Caribbean
caratteristica characteristic
carne (f) meat
　in carne plump
carnevale (m) carnival

caro dear
carta card
　carta di credito credit
　card
casa house
cascina farmhouse
casco helmet
caso case
Caspita! Wow!
castello castle
cattedrale (f) cathedral
cattivo bad, nasty
causa cause
cautela caution
cavallo horse
caviglia ankle
cellulare (m) mobile phone
cena dinner, supper
cenare to have dinner/
supper
centrale central
centro centre
cercare to look for
cerniera zip
certo sure, certain; of
course
che which, who, whom
che? what?
chef (m) chef
chi? who?
chiacchierare to chat
chiamare to call
chiamarsi to be called
chiaramente clearly
chiaro clear
chilometro kilometre
chirurgo surgeon
chiudere to close
chiusura fastening:
chiusura a cerniera zip
ci sono there are
ciao hi, 'bye
cibo food
Cile (m) Chile
Cina China
cinema (m) cinema
cinese Chinese
cioccolato chocolate
cioè i.e./in other words
circa around
circonferenza
circumference
circostante surrounding
città town

classe (f) class
clima (m) climate
climatico climatic
cognato brother-in-law
cognome (m) surname
colazione (f) breakfast
    fare colazione to have
    breakfast
collina hill
    collinare in the hills
colonica: casa colonica
farmhouse
colore (m) colour
coltivazione (f) cultivation
come as
come? how?
cominciare to start
commesso/a shop assistant
comodo comfortable
compagno/a friend,
companion
compatto compact
compilare to fill in (form)
compleanno birthday
complemento
complement
completamente
completely
complimenti
congratulations
complimento compliment
composto made up of
comprare to buy
comprendere to include
comunicare to
communicate
comunicazione (f)
communication
    scienze della
    comunicazione media
    studies
comunque however
con with
condire to season/dress
confermare to confirm
confinare con to border
with
**confusionale: in stato
confusionale** confused
confusione (f) confusion
conoscere to know
(person/place)
conosciuto well-known

conservazione (f)
conservation
consigliabile advisable
consigliare to advise
consulenza advice
contante (m) cash
contatto contact
contenere to contain
contenuto content
continuare to continue
contorno side dish
contro against
controllare to check
contuso bruised
convegno conference
conveniente convenient
coperchio cover, lid
coperto covered
coprire (pp **coperto**) to
cover
corposo full-bodied
corretto correct
corso course
corto short
cosa thing
    (**che**) **cosa?** what?
così so
costare to cost
costo cost
costruire to build
costruttore (m) builder
costruzione (f)
construction
cotone (m) cotton
cotta: avere una cotta per
to have a crush on
cotto cooked
cottura cooking
cozza mussel
cravatta tie
    cravatta a farfalla bow
    tie
crema cream
cretino/a idiot
    fare il cretino to be an
    idiot
cucchiaino teaspoon
cucchiaio spoon
cucciolo puppy
cucina kitchen, cooker,
cuisine
cugino/a cousin
cultura culture
culturale cultural

cuocere to cook
cuore (m) heart
cura cure
curiosità (f) curiosity

D

da from, since
da ... ...'s house
Danimarca Denmark
danza dance
dare (pp **dato**) to give
data date
dati (m pl) data
davvero really
decidere (pp **deciso**) to
decide
definire to define
degustazione (f) tasting
delegato/a delegate
delicato delicate
deluso disappointed
dente (m) tooth
dentista (m/f) dentist
dentro inside
denuncia charge
    fare una denuncia
    to report an incident
descrivere (pp **descritto**)
to describe
descrizione (f) description
desiderare to want
destra right
dettaglio detail
detto said
devastante devastating
di, d' of
di than
dichiarare to declare
dieta diet
dietro behind
dimagrire to lose weight
dimenticare to forget
dimmi (from **dire**) tell me
dire (pp **detto**) to say, tell
direttore (m/f) manager
direttrice (f) manageress
direzione (f) direction,
management
    in direzione di towards
disabile disabled
disastro disaster
discorso speech
discoteca disco
disdetto cancelled

disdire (pp **disdetto**) to cancel
disegno design
dispiace: mi dispiace I'm sorry
dispone di has available
disponibile available
disposizione (f) disposal
distare ... da to be ... away from
Distinti saluti Yours sincerely
disturbo inconvenience
dito (m) finger
   dita (f pl) fingers
divano sofa
   divano letto sofa bed
diventare to become
diverso different, various
divertente funny, amusing
divertirsi to enjoy oneself
diviso divided
divorziato divorced
do (from **dare**) I give
dobbiamo (from **dovere**) we have to
doccia shower
documento document
dolce sweet
dolcelatte Italian cheese
dolore (m) pain
domani tomorrow
domicilio residence
donna woman
dopo after
doppio double
dormire to sleep
dorso back
dosaggio dosage
dotazione: in dotazione supplied
dottore/dottoressa doctor
dove where
dovere to have to, must
dunque so/therefore
duomo cathedral
durante during
durare to last
duro hard

E

è is, lei è you are
e, ed and
ebollizione (f) boiling

eccellente excellent
ecco (t)here (it) is
educato polite
effetto effect
efficace effective
elegante stylish
elenco list
enogastronomia wine and food
entrare to enter
entro by
epoca era
esagerare to exaggerate
esatto exact
   esatto! that's right!
esce, esci, esco, escono (from **uscire** to go out)
escursione (f) tour
esempio example
esercizio exercise
esperienza experience
esplorare to explore
essere to be
est (m) east
estate (f) summer
esterno external
esteso extensive
estetico aesthetic
estremo extreme
eterno eternal
europeo European
evento event
evidentemente evidently

F

fa ago
fa, fai, fanno, fate (from **fare** to do/make)
faccia, faccio, facciamo (from **fare** to do/make)
fagiolino green bean
falso false
fame (f) hunger
   avere fame to be hungry
famiglia family
famoso famous
fantastico fantastic
fare to do, to make
farfalla butterfly
farmacia chemist's
farmacista (m/f) chemist
fatto done
favoloso fabulous

febbre (f) temperature
felpa sweatshirt
femmina female
fermata bus bus stop
festa party
festeggiare to celebrate
fidanzata girlfriend, fiancée
fidanzato boyfriend, fiancé
figlia daughter
figlio son
fine (f) end
finestra window
finire to finish
Finlandia Finland
fino a until
fiore (m) flower
fisicamente physically
foderato lined *(clothes)*
fondo end, bottom
forchetta fork
forma shape
formaggio cheese
fornello cooker
forno oven
forse perhaps
forte strong
fortunatamente fortunately
fortunato fortunate, lucky
foto(grafia) photo(graph)
fra between
   fra un'ora in one hour's time
Francia France
fratello brother
freddo cold
frequentare to attend
fresco chilled
frigo(rifero) fridge
frittata omelette
frontale frontal
fronte (f) front, forehead
   di fronte a opposite
frutta fruit
frutti di mare (m pl) seafood
fuoco fire, gas ring
fuori outside
furto theft

G

galateo etiquette
galleria d'arte art gallery
Galles (m) Wales

gamba leg
gastronomico gastronomic
gelato ice cream
gemelli (m pl) twins
　　letti gemelli twin beds
generale general (adj)
genero son-in-law
genitori (m pl) parents
gentile kind
　　Gentile Signore Dear Sir
Germania Germany
gestire to manage, run
giacca, giacchetta,
giaccone (m) jacket
giallo yellow
Giappone (m) Japan
giapponese Japanese
giardino garden
gilet (m) waistcoat
ginnastica (sing)
gymnastics
ginocchio (m) knee
　　ginocchia (f) knees
giocare to play
giornale (m) newspaper
giornalista (m/f) journalist
giornata day
giorno day
giovane young
　　giovinezza youth
girare to turn
giro tour, trip
giù down
gli (m pl) the, to him/you
godere to enjoy
gola throat
grado degree °C/F
grafico graphic designer
Gran Bretagna Great
Britain
grande big, large
grasso fat
gratis free
grave serious
gravidanza pregnancy
Grecia Greece
greco Greek
grigio grey
gruppo group
guanto glove
guardare to watch
guerra war
guida (m/f) guide
guidato guided
gusto taste

H
ha, hai, hanno, ho (from
avere to have)

I
idea idea
ideale ideal
idraulico plumber
idroterapia hydrotherapy
ieri yesterday
illustratore/trice (m/f)
illustrator
imbottitura padding
immerso immersed
imparare to learn
imperatore (m) emperor
imperiale imperial
impermeabile waterproof
(adj)
importante important
in in, to, by
incidente (m) accident
incluso included, including
incontrare to meet
incredibile incredible
incubo nightmare
indipendente independent
　　casa indipendente
　　detached house
indirizzo address
indossare to wear
infermiere/a nurse
infinito infinite
influenza flu
informazione (f) item of
information
informazioni (f pl)
information, news
Inghilterra England
inglese English
ingresso entrance hall
insieme together
insomma all in all
intelligente intelligent
intenso intense
interessante interesting
interessare to interest
interiore interior
interno internal
invecchiato aged
invernale winter (adj)
inverno winter
inviare to send
invitare to invite

io I
ipertermale hyperthermal
Irlanda Ireland
irlandese Irish
irripetibile unrepeatable
isola island
isolato isolated
istante instant

J
Juventus Turin football
team

L
la (f sing) the, it, her
lana wool
larghezza width
largo wide
lasciare to leave
laterale side (adj)
lavabile washable
lavare to wash
lavastoviglie (f) dishwasher
lavatrice (f) washing
machine
lavorare to work
lavoro job, work
le (f pl) the, them
leggero light
lei you, she, her
lettera letter
letto bed
　　letti a castello bunk beds
　　letti gemelli twin beds
li (m pl) them
lì there
libero free
linea line
lingua language
linguistico linguistic
lino linen
liquido liquid
liquoroso fortified (wine)
liscio straight
lista, listino list
litigare to quarrel, to
squabble
livello level
lo (m sing) the, it
locale (adj) local
locale (m) room
　　locale notturno
　　nightclub
località location, site
Londra London

lontano far
loro they, their, them
lucchetto padlock
lui he, him
lumaca snail
lunghezza length
lungo long
luogo place
  avere luogo to take place

M

ma but
macchina car, machine
macchina fotografica
camera
madre mother
maglia, maglione (m)
sweater
magnifico magnificent,
superb
mai never
malattia illness, disease
male ill
maleducato rude
malissimo dreadfully
mancanza lack
mancare to miss, to be
missing
mandorla almond
mangiare to eat
manica sleeve
mano (f) hand
  mani (f pl) hands
mantenere to maintain
mare (m) sea
marina marine
marito husband
marrone brown
marsupio bum-bag, pouch
marziale martial
maschio male
massaggio massage
massimo maximum
matrimoniale (camera/
letto) double
matrimonio marriage,
wedding
mattina morning
medaglia medal
medicina medicine
medico doctor
medio average
medioevale medieval
meditazione (f) meditation

Mediterraneo
Mediterranean
meglio better (adv)
meno less, least
meraviglia: a meraviglia
superbly
meraviglioso superb,
marvellous
meschino mean
mescolare to mix, to stir
mese (m) month
messaggio message
messo put
metodo method
mettere (pp messo) to put
mezzanotte midnight
mezzo half
mezzogiorno noon, midday
mia, mie, miei, mio my
microonde (m) microwave
miei: i miei my family
migliore better (adj)
minimo minimum
ministro minister
minuto minute
moderno modern
modo way, manner
moglie wife
molto (adj) a lot of, many
molto (adv) very
mondiale world (adj)
mondo world
montagna mountain
montano mountain (adj)
morbido soft
morire (pp morto) to die
moro dark-haired
morto dead
mostra display, exhibition
mostrare to show
motivo reason, motive
motorino scooter
mq square metres
mulino mill
municipale municipal
municipio town hall
muro wall
  i muri walls (of house)
  le mura walls (of city)
museo museum
musica music
  musica lirica opera
musicista (m/f) musician

N

nascere (pp nato) to be
born
nascita birth
naso nose
nato born
natura nature
naturalmente naturally, of
course
nautico nautical, water (adj)
nazionale national
nazionalità nationality
né ... né neither ... nor
ne of it, of them, some, any
nebbia fog
necessario necessary
negoziare to negotiate
negozio shop
nel, nell', nella, nelle in the
nero black
nessuno nobody, anybody
nevicare to snow
nevicata snow shower
niente nothing, anything:
  per niente not at all
nipote (m/f) nephew,
niece, grandchild
nocciola hazelnut
noce (f) nut, walnut
noi we, us
noleggiare to hire
noleggio hire
nome (m) name
non not
nonna grandmother
nonno grandfather
nord (m) north
Norvegia Norway
notizia news item
notturno night (adj)
numero number, shoe size
nuora daughter-in-law
nuotare to swim
nuovo new
nuvola cloud
nuvoloso cloudy

O

o or
occasione occasion,
chance, bargain
occhiali glasses
  occhiali da sole
  sunglasses

occhio eye
oggetto object, e-mail subject
oggi today
ogni each, every
   ogni tanto every so often
olistico holistic
olivo olive, olive tree
ombra shade
omeopatia homeopathy
omeopatico homeopathic
opportunità opportunity
oppure or
opuscolo brochure
ora hour, time
ora now
orario timetable
orecchio ear
organizzare to organise
organizzatore/trice (m/f) organiser
originale original
oro gold
orrendo horrendous
orso bear
ospedale (m) hospital
ospitare to host
ospite (m/f) host, guest
osservare to observe
ottimo excellent
ovest (m) west

P

pacchetto parcel, packet
pace (f) peace
padella pan
paesaggio landscape
paese (m) country, village
Paesi Bassi (m pl) Netherlands
pagare to pay (for)
paio pair
palazzo apartment block, palace
palestra gym
paletta (cooking) slice
pallavolo volleyball
palma palm
palmare (m) palmtop
panino bread roll
panna dairy cream
panoramico scenic
pantalone (m sing) trousers
paragonare to compare

parapendio paragliding
parcheggiare to park
parcheggio carpark
parco park
parlare to speak, talk
parte (f) part
partecipare to take part
partire to depart, to leave
partita match
parzialmente partially
Pasqua Easter
passatempo hobby
passeggiare to walk
passione (f) passion
passo step
   a due passi very near
pasto meal
patate novelle new potatoes
patente (f) di guida driving licence
pattuglia della polizia police patrol (car)
paura fear
   avere paura to be afraid
pausa break: fare una pausa to have a break
pazzo crazy
peccato pity, sin
pecorino ewe's cheese
pelle (f) skin, leather
pelliccia fur
pendolare: fare il/la pendolare to commute
pensare to think
pentola saucepan
pepe (m) pepper
per for, in order to
perché because, why?
perdente (m/f) loser
perdere to lose
perfettamente perfectly
perfetto perfect
perfezione (f) perfection
periferia suburb, outskirts
periodo period of time
permanenza
   Buona permanenza! Enjoy your stay!
però but, however
persona person
personale (m) personnel
personale personal
personalizzato

personalised
pesca peach
pesce (m) fish
pessimo dreadful
pezzo, pezzettino piece
piacere (m) pleasure
piacere to please
piaciuto liked
piano floor
   piano terra ground floor
pianta, piantina map
piatto plate, dish, course
piccolo small, little
piede (m) foot
piegare to bend
pieno full
pietra stone
pinguino penguin
pioggia rain
piovere to rain
piscina swimming pool
pista track, (ski) slope
pittura painting
più more, most
piuttosto rather
po': un po' (adv) a bit
poco (adv) a little, a few; (adv) not very
poi then
polacco Polish
polizia police
poliziotto policeman
Polonia Poland
polso wrist
pomeriggio afternoon
ponte (m) bridge
porcini (m pl) mushrooms
porgere to offer
portafogli(o) wallet, purse
portare to wear, carry
portatile (m) laptop
Portogallo Portugal
posizione (f) position
possibilità possibility
posso, possiamo, possono (from potere to be able to)
postino postman
posto place
potere to be able to, can
povero poor
   Poverino/a! You poor thing!
pranzare to have lunch
pranzo lunch

praticamente practically, in practice
pratico practical
precisamente precisely
preferibilmente preferably
preferire to prefer
preferito favourite
preistorico prehistoric
prelevare to withdraw (cash)
prendere (pp preso) to take
prenotare to book
prenotazione booking
preparare to prepare
presentare to introduce
preso taken
presso near, at
presto early
prevalentemente predominantly
previsioni (f pl) meteo weather forecast
prezzo price
prima possibile as soon as possible
primo first
principale principal, main
principalmente mainly
problema (m) problem
prodotto product
professionale professional
professione (f) profession
profondità depth
programmatore/trice (m/f) programmer
pronto ready, Hello (phone)
pronto soccorso first aid, casualty department
proprietà property
proprietario/a proprietor
proprio (adj) one's own
proprio (adv) really
prosciutto ham
prossimità proximity
prossimo next
provare to try (on)
provincia province
pulire to clean
punto di vista point of view
può, puoi (from potere to be able to)
puro pure

Q

qualche some, a few
qualcosa something
qualcuno somebody
quale which
qualità quality
quando when, when
quanti/e? how many?
quantità quantity
quanto/a? how much?
quarto quarter
quasi almost
quello that
questo this
questura police station
qui here
    qui vicino round here
quindi so/therefore

R

raccomandare to recommend
    Mi raccomando! For goodness sake!
radicchio type of lettuce
raffinatezza refinement
ragazza girl, girlfriend
ragazzo boy, boyfriend
ragionevole reasonable
rapidamente quickly
rapido quick
recente recent
regionale regional
regione (f) region
Regno Unito UK
regola rule
regolarmente regularly
reputazione (f) reputation
residente (m/f) resident
responsabile responsible, in charge
restare to stay
restaurare to restore
restaurato restored
ricchezza richness
riccio curly
ricco rich
ricetta recipe
ricevere to receive
richiesta request
ricordare to remember, remind
ridicolo ridiculous

rilasciare to issue (document)
rilassante relaxing
rimanere to remain
rinforzato reinforced
riposarsi to rest
riprendere to resume
riscaldamento heating
riscaldare to heat
rischio risk
riserva reserve
rispondere to answer
risposta reply
ristorante (m) restaurant
ristrutturare to refurbish, renovate
risultato result
ritardo: in ritardo late
ritornare to return
riunire to gather
riunirsi to get together
riuscire to succeed in
robusto robust
rosa rose, pink
rosato rosé (wine)
rosmarino rosemary
rosso red
rotella roller
rotto broken
rurale rural
rustico country pad, rustic

S

sacco bag
sagra food/wine festival
sala room
    sala da pranzo dining room
salato salty
sale (m) salt
salire to come/go up
salone (m) lounge
salsa sauce
salute (f) health
saluto greeting
    Distinti saluti Yours faithfully, sincerely
sangue (m) blood
sapere to know (facts)
sapore (m) flavour
sarà (from essere) will be
sardo Sardinian
sasso rock

sbagliare to mistake, to be wrong
sbattere to beat
scaldare to heat
scalino step, stair
scambiare to exchange
scamosciato suede (adj)
scarpa shoe
scarponcini da trekking (m pl) walking boots
scegliere to choose
scendere (pp sceso) to come/go down, to get off
schiena back
schiera terrace
sci (m) ski
scienza science
scienziato/a scientist
scodella bowl
scolare to drain
sconto discount
scoprire to discover
scorso last
Scozia Scotland
scrivere (pp scritto) to write
scuro dark
scusare to excuse
scusarsi to apologise
se if
secco dry
secondo (adj) second; according to
segreto secret
seguire to follow
sei (from essere) you are
sei six
semaforo (sing) traffic lights
seminario seminar
semplice simple
semplicemente simply
sempre always, still
sentiero path, walk
senza without
    senz'altro of course
sera evening
servire to serve
servizio service
seta silk
Settecento 18th century
settentrionale northern
settimana week
settimanale weekly

settore (m) sector
sfortunatamente unfortunately
sì yes
Sicilia Sicily
sicuro safe
silenzio silence
simpatico nice
singolo single
sinistra left
sintomo symptom
slogarsi to sprain
smarrimento loss
smarrire to lose
smeraldo emerald
snello slim
so (from sapere) I know
sobbollire to simmer
soffrire to suffer
soggiorno holiday; living-room
sole (m) sun
soleggiato sunny
solito usual
    di solito usually
solo only
    da solo on one's own
soltanto only
sondaggio survey
sono (from essere) I am, they are
soprattutto especially
sorella sister
sorridere to smile
sotto under
Spagna Spain
spalla shoulder
spazioso spacious
specialità speciality
spedire to send
spento dull, pale
sperare to hope
spesso often
spettacolare spectacular
spettacolo spectacle
spiaggia beach
spiegare to explain
spinaci (m pl) spinach
splendido splendid
sport (m) sport(s)
sportello window, counter
sportivo casual
sposarsi to get married
sposato married

spumante (m) sparkling (wine)
squadra team
squisito exquisite, gorgeous
stanco tired
stanza room
stare to be
Stati Uniti (m pl) USA
stato (pp of essere and stare) been
stazione (f) station
stesso same, self
stile (m) style
stilista (m/f) fashion designer
stivale (m) boot
stomaco stomach
storia history, story
storico historical
stoviglie (f pl) dishes
strada road, street
stradale road (adj)
stradina lane
stragrande ultra large
straordinario extraordinary
straricco ultra rich
strasimpatico extremely nice
stravagante extravagant, unconventional
stressato stressed
stretto tight
studente/tessa (m/f) student
studiare to study
stupendo superb
su on, up
subacqueo underwater
subito suddenly, immediately
succedere (pp successo) to happen
successo: cos'è successo? what (has) happened?
sud (m) south
Sudafrica South Africa
sugo sauce
suo, sua, sue, suoi his, her, its, your (lei)
suocera mother-in-law
superare to go over, to overcome
superiore superior

supermercato supermarket
svegliarsi to wake up
Svezia Sweden
sviluppare to develop
Svizzera Switzerland

T

taglia size
Tailandia Thailand
tanti/e so many
tanto/a so much
tardi late
tasca pocket
tavola, tavolo table
telefonare to phone
telefonino mobile phone
telefono phone
televisione (f) television
temperatura ambiente
room temperature
tempio temple
tempo time, weather
temporale (m) storm
tenere to hold
tenero tender
terapeutico therapeutic
termale thermal, spa (adj)
terme (f pl) spa, thermal
baths
terra earth, floor
terrazzo terrace
terreno land
terzo third
teso uptight, strained
tesoro treasure
tessuto fabric
testa head
tifoso/a fan
tipo type
tiramisù Italian dessert
tizio bloke
togliere to remove
torcia torch
tornare to return
torre (f) tower
torta cake
tosse (f) cough
totalmente totally
tradizionale traditional
traghetto ferry
tragico tragic
tranquillità tranquility
tranquillo peaceful
trascorrere to spend *(time)*

trasporto transport
trattamento treatment
trattare to treat
trattoria restaurant
trauma (m) trauma
treno train
triste sad
troppo (adj) too much/
many
troppo (adv) too
trovare to find
trovarsi to be located
tu you
tuo, tua, tue, tuoi your
Turchia Turkey
turismo tourism
turistico touristic
tutto all

U

ufficio postale post office
ultimo last
Ungheria Hungary
università university
uovo (m) egg
  uova (f pl) eggs
urbano urban
usare to use
uscire to go out
uso use
utile useful

V

va bene OK
vacanza holiday
vado, vai, va, vanno (from
andare to go)
validità validity
vallata hollow
valore (m) value
vario various
vasellame (m) china
vecchio old
vedere (pp visto) to see
  non vedere l'ora to look
  forward
vedova/o widow(er)
vela: fare la vela to sail
vendere to sell
vendesi for sale
venire to come
vento wind
veramente truly, really
verde green

verdura vegetable
vergine (f) virgin
vero true, real
versare to pour
versione (f) version
verso towards
vestirsi to get dressed
vestito dress
viaggiare to travel
viaggio journey
vicino near; neighbour
vigna, vigneto vineyard
villa house, villa
villaggio village
villetta a schiera terraced
house
vincere (pp vinto) to win
vincitore/trice (m/f) winner
vino wine
vinto won
viola violet
visitare to visit
viso face
vista view
visto (from vedere) seen
vita life, waist
vittoria victory
vivace bright, lively
vivacemente briskly, in a
lively way
vivere (pp vissuto) to live
voglia wish
  avere voglia di to feel like
voglio (from volere to
want)
voi you (pl)
volentieri with pleasure
volo flight
vorrebbe you (lei) would
like
vorrei/vorremmo I/we
would like
vostro your
vuoi, vuole (from volere
to want)

Z

zaino, zainetto backpack
zia aunt
zio uncle
zona area
zucchino courgette

English–Italian glossary

A

able: to be able to **potere**
absolutely **assolutamente**
access **accesso**
accessory **accessorio**
accident **incidente** (m)
accommodation **alloggio**
according to **secondo**
actor **attore/attrice** (m/f)
acupuncture **agopuntura**
to add **aggiungere**
address **indirizzo**
to admire **ammirare**
adventure **avventura**
advice **consiglio,
consulenza**
advisable **consigliabile**
to advise **consigliare**
affectionate **affettuoso**
afraid: to be afraid **avere
paura**
after **dopo**
afternoon **pomeriggio**
again **ancora**
against **contro**
aged **invecchiato**
agricultural **agricolo**
airport **aeroporto**
alcohol **alcol** (m)
alcoholic **alcolico**
all **tutto**
allergic **allergico**
almond **mandorla**
almost **quasi**
also **anche**
always **sempre**
amusing **divertente**
analyst **analista** (m/f)
anchovy **alice** (f)
ancient **antico**
and **e, ed**
ankle **caviglia**
anniversary **anniversario**
to answer **rispondere**
antiquated **antiquato**
antique (adj) **antico**
anybody **qualcuno**
anything **qualcosa**
appointment
appuntamento

archaeologist **archeologo**
architect **architetto**
area **zona**
arm **braccio** (m)
    arms **le braccia** (fpl)
around **circa**
to arrive **arrivare**
art **arte** (f)
arthritis **artrite** (f)
article **articolo**
to assume **assumere**
asthma **asma**
at **a**
to attend **frequentare**
aunt **zia**
available **disponibile**
average **medio**
away: to be ... away **distare**
Azores **Azzorre** (fpl)

B

baby **bambino/a**
back **dorso, schiena**
backpack **zaino, zainetto**
balanced **bilanciato**
balcony **balcone** (m)
bank **banca**
banker **banchiere** (m)
bargain **affare** (m)
bath **bagno**
bathroom **bagno**
to be **essere, stare**
beach **spiaggia**
bean (green) **fagiolino**
bear **orso**
to beat **sbattere**
beautiful **bello**
because **perché**
bed **letto**
to begin **cominciare**
behind **dietro**
Belgium **Belgio**
to bend **piegare**
beneficial **benefico**
better **migliore** (adj),
meglio (adv)
between **fra, tra**
big **grande**
bike **bici** (f), **bicicletta**
binoculars **binocolo** (sing)

birth **nascita**
birthday **compleanno**
bit (a) **un po'**
black **nero**
block (of flats) **palazzo**
bloke **tizio**
blonde **biondo**
blood **sangue** (m)
blue **azzurro, blu**
to boil **bollire**
boiling **ebollizione** (f)
to book **prenotare**
booking **prenotazione** (f)
boot **stivale** (m)
to border with **confinare
con**
born: to be born **nascere**
(pp **nato**)
bottom **fondo**
bowl **scodella**
boy **ragazzo**
boyfriend **ragazzo,
fidanzato**
break **pausa**
to break **rompere** (pp
rotto)
breakfast **colazione** (f)
bridge **ponte** (m)
bright **vivace**
brochure **opuscolo**
brother **fratello**
brother-in-law **cognato**
brown **marrone, bruno**
to browse **guardare**
bruised **contuso**
builder **costruttore** (m)
bumbag **marsupio**
bunk beds **letti a castello**
burner **fornello, fuoco**
bus **autobus** (m)
bus stop **fermata bus**
but **ma, però**
butter **burro**
to buy **comprare**
by (date) **entro**

C

cake **torta**
calendar **calendario**
to call **chiamare**

called: to be called **chiamarsi**

camera **macchina fotografica**

campsite **campeggio**

can (to be able to) **potere**

to cancel **disdire** (pp **disdetto**)

capacious **capiente**

capsule **capsula**

car **macchina, auto** (f)

Caribbean **Caraibi** (m pl)

car park **parcheggio**

to carry on **continuare**

to carry **portare**

cash **contante** (m)

cashpoint **bancomat** (m)

cashmere **cachemire** (m)

castle **castello**

casualty department **pronto soccorso**

cat **gatto**

to catch (train) **prendere**

cathedral **duomo, cattedrale** (f)

cause **causa**

to celebrate **festeggiare**

cellar **cantina**

central **centrale**

centre **centro**

certain **certo**

chance **opportunità**

change **cambiamento**

to change **cambiare**

characteristic **caratteristico**

charge: in charge **responsabile**

to chat **chiacchierare**

to check **controllare**

cheerful **allegro**

cheese **formaggio**

chemist **farmacista** (m/f)

chemist's **farmacia**

championships **campionati** (m pl)

Chile **Cile** (m)

chilled **fresco**

China **Cina**

china **vasellame** (m)

Chinese **cinese**

chocolate **cioccolato**

to choose **scegliere**

circumference **circonferenza**

class **classe** (f)

clear **chiaro**

clearly **chiaramente**

climate **clima** (m), **climatico** (adj)

to close **chiudere**

cloud **nuvola**

cloudy **nuvoloso**

coffee **caffè** (m)

cold **freddo**

to be cold **avere freddo**

colour **colore** (m)

to come **venire** (pp **venuto**)

to come down **scendere** (pp **sceso**)

to come up **salire**

comfortable **comodo**

to communicate **comunicare**

to commute **fare il/la pendolare**

compact **compatto**

companion **compagno/a**

to compare **paragonare**

compass **bussola**

completely **completamente**

compliment **complimento**

to comprise **comprendere**

conference **convegno**

to confirm **confermare**

confused **in stato confusionale**

confusion **confusione** (f)

congratulations **complimenti** (m pl)

conservation **conservazione** (f)

construction **costruzione** (f)

contact **contatto**

to contain **contenere**

contents **contenuti** (m pl)

convenient **comodo, conveniente**

to cook **cuocere** (pp **cotto**)

cooker **cucina, fornello**

cooking **cucina, cottura**

cool **fresco**

corner **angolo**

correct **corretto**

to cost **costare**

cotton **cotone** (m)

cough **tosse** (f)

country **paese** (m)

countryside **campagna**

course **corso, piatto**

course: of course **certo, naturalmente**

cousin **cugino/a**

cover **coperchio, copertura**

to cover **coprire** (pp **coperto**)

crazy **pazzo**

to cross **attraversare**

crush: to have a crush on **avere una cotta per**

cuisine **cucina**

cultural **culturale**

culture **cultura**

cure **cura**

curiosity **curiosità**

curly **riccio**

currently **attualmente**

D

dance **danza**

dark **scuro**

dark-haired **moro**

data **dati** (m pl)

date **data, appuntamento**

daughter **figlia**

daughter-in-law **nuora**

day **giorno, giornata**

dead **morto**

dear **caro**

Dear Sir **Gentile Signore**

to decide **decidere** (pp **deciso**)

to declare **dichiarare**

to define **definire**

degree (°C/F) **grado**

degree (academic) **laurea**

delegate **delegato/a**

delicate **delicato**

demonstration **mostra**

dentist **dentista** (m/f)

to depart **partire**

depth **profondità**

to descend **scendere** (pp **sceso**)

to describe **descrivere** (pp **descritto**)

description **descrizione** (f)

design **disegno**

designer **grafico, stilista** (m/f)

detached **indipendente,**

monofamiliare
detail **dettaglio**
devastating **devastante**
to develop **sviluppare**
to die **morire** (pp **morto**)
diet **dieta**
different **diverso**
to dine **cenare**
dining room **sala da pranzo**
dinner **cena**
disabled **disabile**
disagreeable **antipatico**
disappointed **deluso**
disaster **disastro**
disco **discoteca**
discount **sconto**
to discover **scoprire**
disease **malattia**
dish **piatto**
dishes **stoviglie** (fpl)
dishwasher **lavastoviglie** (f)
divorced **divorziato**
to do **fare** (pp **fatto**)
doctor **medico, dottore** (m/f)
dog **cane** (m)
dosage **dosaggio**
double **doppio**
down **giù**
to drain **scolare**
dreadful **pessimo**
dreadfully **malissimo**
dream **sogno**
to dress **vestirsi**
dress **vestito**
driving licence **patente** (f) **di guida**
dry **secco**
dryer *(clothes)* **asciugabiancheria**
during **durante**

E
each **ogni**
ear **orecchio**
early **presto**
east **est** (m)
Easter **Pasqua**
to eat **mangiare**
effect **effetto**
effective **efficace**
egg **uovo** (m)
    eggs **uova** (fpl)

emerald **smeraldo**
emperor **imperatore**
end **fine** (f)
England **Inghilterra**
English **inglese**
to enjoy **godere**
to enjoy oneself **divertirsi**
enough **abbastanza**
entrance hall **ingresso, atrio**
equipped **attrezzato**
especially **soprattutto**
estate agent/agency **agente/agenzia immobiliare**
eternal **eterno**
etiquette **galateo**
EU **UE: Unione Europea**
European **europeo**
even **anche**
evening **sera**
event **evento**
every **ogni**
every so often **ogni tanto**
evidently **evidentemente**
exact **esatto**
to exaggerate **esagerare**
example **esempio**
to exceed **superare**
excellent **eccellente, ottimo**
exchange **scambiare**
exercise **esercizio**
exhibition **mostra**
expensive **caro**
experience **esperienza**
to explain **spiegare**
to explore **esplorare**
exquisite **squisito**
extensive **esteso**
external **esterno**
extravagant **stravagante**
extreme **estremo**
eye **occhio**

F
fabric **tessuto**
fabulous **favoloso**
face **viso**
faithfully: Yours faithfully **Distinti saluti**
to fall **cadere**
false **falso**
family **famiglia**

famous **conosciuto, famoso**
fan **tifoso**
fantastic **fantastico**
far **lontano**
    as far as **fino a**
farmhouse **cascina, casa colonica**
fashion **moda**
    fashion designer **stilista**
fastening **chiusura**
fat **grasso**
favourite **preferito**
to fear **avere paura**
fear **paura**
female **femmina**
ferry **traghetto**
festival **festa, sagra**
fever **febbre** (f)
few **pochi/e**
few: a few **alcuni/e**
fiancé(e) **fidanzato/a**
to fill (in) **compilare**
to find **trovare**
finger **dito** (m)
    fingers **dita** (fpl)
to finish **finire**
Finland **Finlandia**
fire **fuoco**
fireplace **camino, caminetto**
first aid **pronto soccorso**
first **primo**
fish **pesce** (m)
flat **appartamento**
flavour **sapore** (m)
flight **volo**
floor **piano**
flower **fiore** (m)
flu **influenza**
fog **nebbia**
to follow **seguire**
food **cibo**
foot **piede** (m)
football **calcio**
for **per, da**
forehead **fronte** (f)
to forget **dimenticare**
fork **forchetta**
fortified (wine) **liquoroso**
fortunate **fortunato**
fortunately **fortunatamente**
forward: to look forward **non vedere l'ora**

France Francia
free *(no cost)* libero, gratis
fridge frigo(rifero)
friend amico/a
from da
fruit frutta
full pieno
full-bodied *(wine)* corposo
funny comico, divertente
fur pelliccia
furnished arredato

G

gallery galleria
garage box, garage (m)
garden giardino
general generale
Germany Germania
to get off scendere (pp sceso)
to get on salire
to get up alzarsi
girl ragazza
girlfriend ragazza, fidanzata
glass bicchiere (m)
glasses occhiali (m pl)
glove guanto
to go andare
to go back (ri)tornare
to go down scendere (pp sceso)
to go in entrare
to go out uscire
to go up salire
gold oro
golf course campo da golf
good buono, bravo
goodbye arrivederci
gourmet buongustaio
grandchild nipote (m/f)
grandfather nonno
grandmother nonna
great grande
Great Britain Gran Bretagna
great-grandfather bisnonno
great-grandmother bisnonna
Greece Grecia
Greek greco
green verde
greeting augurio, saluto

greetings card biglietto di auguri
grey grigio
ground terra
group gruppo
guest ospite (m/f)
guide guida
gym palestra
gymnastics ginnastica (sing)

H

hair capelli (m pl)
half mezzo
hall entrata, vestibolo
ham prosciutto
hand mano (f)
   hands mani (fpl)
handbag borsetta
to happen succedere
hard duro
hat cappello
to have avere
to have to dovere
hazel nocciola
he lui
head testa, capo
health salute (f)
heart cuore (m)
to heat (ri)scaldare
heat calore (m)
heating riscaldamento
height altezza
hello buongiorno
   (answering phone) pronto
helmet casco
to help aiutare
help aiuto
her la, lei, suo/a
here qui
   here is/are ecco
hill collina
him lo, lui
to hire noleggiare
his suo
historical storico
history storia
hobby passatempo
holdall borsone (m)
holiday soggiorno, vacanza
holistic olistico
hollow vallata
home casa, domicilio

homeopathic omeopatico
hood cappuccio
to hope sperare
horrendous orrendo
horse cavallo
hospital ospedale (m)
to host ospitare
host ospite (m/f)
hot caldo
to be hot avere caldo
hour ora
house casa
how che
   how lovely che bello
how? come?
   how many? quanti/e?
   how much? quanto/a?
however comunque, però
to hug abbracciare
hug abbraccio
huge enorme, stragrande
Hungary Ungheria
hungry: to be hungry avere fame
to hurt avere/fare male
husband marito
hypermarket ipermercato

I

I io
i.e. cioè
idea idea
ideal ideale
idiot cretino
if se
to be ill stare male
illness malattia
immediately subito
important importante
in a, in
included compreso, incluso
inconvenience disturbo
incredible incredibile
independent indipendente
information informazioni (fpl)
inside dentro
instant attimo, istante (m)
insurance assicurazione (f)
intelligent intelligente
intense intenso
to interest interessare
interesting interessante

interior **interiore** (m)
internal **interno**
to introduce **presentare**
to invite **invitare**
Ireland **Irlanda**
Irish **irlandese**
is **è**
island **isola**
isolated **isolato**

J

jacket **giacca, giacchetta**
Japan **Giappone** (m)
Japanese **giapponese**
journalist **giornalista** (m/f)
journey **viaggio**
jumper **maglia**

K

kilometre **chilometro**
kind **gentile**
kiss **bacio**
kitchen **cucina**
knee **ginocchio** (m)
   knees **ginocchia** (fpl)
knife **coltello**
to know *(fact)* **sapere**
(person/place) **conoscere**

L

lack **mancanza**
to lack **mancare**
lamb **agnello**
land **terreno**
landscape **paesaggio**
language **lingua**
laptop **portatile** (m)
large **ampio, grande**
to last **durare**
last **scorso, ultimo**
late *(behind time)* **tardi, in
ritardo**
lawyer **avvocato**
to learn **imparare**
least **minimo**
   at least **almeno**
leather **cuoio, pelle** (f)
to leave **lasciare, partire**
left **sinistra**
leg **gamba**
length **lunghezza**
less **meno**
letter **lettera**
level **livello**

lid **coperchio**
life **vita**
lift **ascensore** (m)
light **leggero**
light **luce** (f)
to like **piacere a** (pp
piaciuto)
lined *(clothes)* **foderato**
linen **lino**
linguistic **linguistico**
liquid **liquido**
list **elenco, lista, listino**
little **piccolo**
to live **abitare, vivere**
lively **vivace**
local **locale**
London **Londra**
long **lungo**
to look at **guardare**
to look for **cercare**
to lose **perdere, smarrire**
loser **perdente** (m/f)
loss **smarrimento**
lot: a lot of **molto**
lounge **salone** (m),
soggiorno
lucky **fortunato, beato**
to have lunch **pranzare**
lunch **pranzo**

M

mad **matto, pazzo**
magnificent **magnifico**
mainly **principalmente**
to maintain **mantenere**
to make **fare** (pp **fatto**)
male **maschio**
to manage to **riuscire a**
manager **direttore** (m/f)
manageress **direttrice**
many **molti/e**
map **mappa, pianta,
piantina**
marine (adj) **marina/o**
marriage **matrimonio**
married **sposato**
to get married **sposarsi**
martial arts **arti marziali**
(fpl)
marvellous **meraviglioso**
massage **massaggio**
masterpiece **capolavoro**
match *(sport)* **partita**
to match **abbinare**

maximum **massimo**
me **me, mi**
meal **pasto**
mean **meschino**
to mean **volere dire**
meat **carne** (f)
medal **medaglia**
media studies **scienze della
comunicazione** (fpl)
medicine **medicina**
medieval **medioevale**
meditation **meditazione** (f)
medium-sweet *(wine)*
amabile
to meet **incontrare**
to meet up **riunire**
message **messaggio**
microwave **microonde** (m)
midday **mezzogiorno**
midnight **mezzanotte** (f)
mill **mulino**
mimimum **minimo**
minister **ministro**
minute **minuto**
to miss **mancare**
mist **foschia**
to mistake **sbagliare**
to mix **mescolare**
mobile phone **cellulare**
(m), **telefonino**
modern **moderno**
moment **attimo, momento**
month **mese** (m)
more **più**
morning **mattina**
most **il più**
mother **madre**
mother-in-law **suocera**
mountain **montagna,
montano** (adj)
moustache **baffi** (m pl)
mouth **bocca**
municipal **municipale**
museum **museo**
music **musica**
musician **musicista** (m/f)
mussel **cozza**
must: to have to **dovere**
my **mio**

N

name **nome** (m)
nasty **cattivo**
national **nazionale**

nationality **nazionalità**
naturally **naturalmente**
nature **natura**
nautical **nautico**
navy **blu**
near **vicino**
nearly **quasi**
necessary **necessario**
   it's necessary **bisogna**
need **bisogno**
to need **avere bisogno di**
to negotiate **negoziare**
neither ... nor **né ... né**
nephew **nipote**
Netherlands **Paesi Bassi**
never **mai**
new **nuovo**
   new potatoes **patate novelle** (fpl)
New Zealand **Nuova Zelanda**
news **notizie** (fpl)
newspaper **giornale** (m)
next **prossimo**
next to **accanto**
nice **simpatico**
niece **nipote**
night **notte** (f), **notturno** (adj)
nightclub **locale notturno**
nightmare **incubo**
nobody **nessuno**
noon **mezzogiorno**
north **nord** (m)
Norway **Norvegia**
nose **naso**
note **banconota**
nothing **niente**
now **ora, adesso, attualmente**
nurse **infermiere/a**
nut **noce**

O
object **oggetto**
to observe **osservare**
occasion **occasione** (f)
occasionally **ogni tanto**
of course **senz'altro, certo**
of **di**
office **ufficio**
often **spesso**
OK **d'accordo, va bene**
old **vecchio**

olive **olivo**
olive tree **olivo**
omelette **frittata**
on **su**
one-off **irripetibile**
only **solo, soltanto**
open **aperto**
   open air **all'aperto**
to open **aprire**
opening **apertura**
opera **musica lirica**
opinion **punto di vista**
   in my opinion **secondo me**
opportunity **opportunità**
opposite **di fronte a**
or **o, oppure**
to organise **organizzare**
original **originale**
other **altro**
our **nostro**
outside **fuori**
outskirts **periferia** (f sing)
oven **forno**
own **proprio**
   on one's own **da solo**
   one's own (adj) **proprio**
owner **proprietario/a**

P
packet **pacchetto**
padlock **lucchetto**
pain **dolore** (m)
painkiller **antidolorifico**
painting **pittura**
pair **paio**
palace **palazzo**
pale **spento, chiaro** (colour)
pan **padella, pentola**
paragliding **parapendio**
parcel **pacchetto**
parents **genitori** (m pl)
to park **parcheggiare**
park **parco**
parmesan **parmigiano**
part **parte** (f)
partially **parzialmente**
participate **partecipare**
party **festa**
passion **passione** (f)
path **sentiero**
to pay (for) **pagare**
peace **pace** (f) **tranquillità**
peaceful **tranquillo**

peach **pesca**
penguin **pinguino**
pepper **pepe** (m)
perfect **perfetto**
perfection **perfezione** (f)
perfectly **perfettamente**
perhaps **forse**
period **periodo**
person **persona**
personal **personale**
to phone **telefonare**
photo(graph) **foto(grafia)**
physically **fisicamente**
piece **pezzo, pezzettino**
pink **rosa**
pity **peccato**
place **posto, luogo**
to take place **avere luogo**
plate **piatto**
to play **giocare**
please **per favore/piacere**
to please **piacere a**
pleasure **piacere**
plumber **idraulico**
plump **in carne**
pocket **tasca**
point of view **punto di vista**
Poland **Polonia**
police **Polizia, Carabinieri** (m pl)
police officer **agente di polizia, poliziotto**
police station **questura**
Polish **polacco**
polite **educato**
pool **piscina**
poor **povero**
Portugal **Portogallo**
position **posizione** (f)
possibility **possibilità**
postman **postino**
pot **pentola**
potato **patata**
to pour **versare**
practical **pratico**
practically **praticamente**
precise **preciso**
precisely **precisamente**
to prefer **preferire**
preferably **preferibilmente**
pregnancy **gravidanza**
pregnant **incinta**
prehistoric **preistorico**

to prepare preparare
to present presentare
press stampa
price prezzo
principal principale
problem problema (m)
product prodotto
profession professione (f)
professional professionale
programmer programmatore/trice (m/f)
property proprietà
proprietor proprietario/a
puppy cucciolo
pure puro
purse portafogli(o) (m)
to put mettere
to put down appoggiare

Q

quality qualità
quantity quantità
to quarrel litigare
quarter quarto
quick rapido
quickly rapidamente
quiet tranquillo
quite abbastanza

R

rain pioggia
to rain piovere
rapidly rapidamente
rather piuttosto
real vero
really davvero, veramente, (adv) proprio
reason motivo
reasonable ragionevole
to receive ricevere
recent recente
recipe ricetta
to recommend raccomandare
red rosso
refinement raffinatezza
to refurbish ristrutturare
region regione (f)
regional regionale
regularly regolarmente
relaxing rilassante
to remember ricordare
to remind ricordare
to remove togliere

to rent prendere in affitto
to rent out affittare
to reply rispondere
reply risposta
to report fare una denuncia
reputation reputazione (f)
request richiesta
reservation prenotazione (f)
resident residente (m/f)
responsible responsabile
to rest riposarsi
restaurant ristorante (m)
to restore restaurare
result risultato
to resume riprendere
to return (ri)tornare
rich ricco
ridiculous ridicolo
right destra
risk rischio
road strada, (adj) stradale
roasted arrosto
robust robusto
rock sasso
roller rotella
room stanza, sala, locale, camera
rose rosa
rosé rosato
rosemary rosmarino
rude maleducato
rule regola
rural rurale

S

sad triste
safe sicuro
to sail fare la vela
salt sale (m)
salty salato
same stesso
sauce salsa, sugo
saucepan pentola
to say dire (pp detto)
scientist scienziato/a
scooter motorino
Scotland Scozia
sea mare (m)
seafood frutti (m pl) di mare
to season condire
secret segreto

sector settore (m)
to see vedere
to sell vendere
semi-detached bifamiliare
seminar seminario
to send inviare, mandare, spedire
serious grave
to serve servire
service servizio
shade ombra
shape forma
shirt camicia
shoe scarpa
shop assistant commesso/a
shop negozio
short basso, corto, breve
shoulder spalla
to show mostrare
show spettacolo
shower *(rain)* acquazzone (m)
shower doccia
to shut chiudere
side (adj) laterale
    side dish contorno
silence silenzio
silk seta
silver argento
to simmer sobbollire
simple semplice
simply semplicemente
sin peccato
sincerely: Yours sincerely Distinti saluti
singer cantante (m/f)
single singolo
sister sorella
size taglia, numero
ski sci (m)
to ski sciare
skin pelle (f)
to sleep dormire
sleeve manica
slim snello
small piccolo
to smile sorridere
snail lumaca
snow neve (f)
to snow nevicare
so così, dunque, quindi
sofa divano
    sofa bed divano letto
soft morbido

something **qualcosa**
sometimes **qualche volta**
son **figlio**
son-in-law **genero**
soon **fra poco**
    as soon as possible
    prima possibile
sorry **mi dispiace**
South Africa **Sudafrica**
south **sud** (m)
spa **terme** (fpl)
spacious **spazioso**
Spain **Spagna**
sparkling *(wine)* **spumante**
to speak **parlare**
speciality **specialità**
spectacular **spettacolare**
speech **discorso**
to spend *(time)* **trascorrere**
splendid **splendido**
spoon **cucchiaio**
to sprain **slogarsi**
to squabble **litigare**
stair **scalino**
to start **cominciare**
station **stazione** (f)
to stay **restare**
step **passo**
still **ancora, sempre**
to stir **mescolare**
stomach **stomaco**
stone **pietra**
storm **temporale** (m)
straight *(hair)* **liscio**
straightaway **subito**
stressed **stressato**
strong **forte**
student **studente/tessa** (m/f)
to study **studiare**
style **stile** (m)
stylish **elegante**
subject *(e-mail)* **oggetto**
suburb **periferia**
to succeed **riuscire**
suddenly **subito**
suede **scamosciato**
to suffer **soffrire**
suitable **adatto**
summer **estate** (f)
sun **sole** (m)
sunglasses **occhiali da sole** (m pl)
sunny **soleggiato**
superb **meraviglioso,**

stupendo
superior **superiore**
supermarket **supermercato**
supper **cena**
sure **certo, sicuro**
surgeon **chirurgo**
surname **cognome** (m)
surrounding (adj) **circostante**
survey **sondaggio**
sweater **maglia, maglione** (m)
sweatshirt **felpa**
Sweden **Svezia**
sweet **dolce**
to swim **nuotare**
swimming pool **piscina**
Switzerland **Svizzera**
symptom **sintomo**

T

table **tavola, tavolo**
to take **prendere**
to talk **parlare**
tall **alto**
to taste **assaggiare**
taste **gusto**
tasting **degustazione** (f)
team **squadra**
teaspoon **cucchiaino**
to telephone **telefonare**
telephone **telefono**
television **televisione** (f)
to tell **dire** (pp **detto**)
temperature **temperatura, febbre** (f)
    at room temperature **a temperatura ambiente**
temple **tempio**
tender **tenero**
terrace **terrazza, terrazzo**
terraced **a schiera**
Thailand **Tailandia**
than **di**
that **quello**
the **il, la, l', lo, i, le, gli**
theft **furto**
their **loro**
them **li, le, loro**
then **poi**
therapeutic **terapeutico**
there are **ci sono**
there is **c'è**
there **lì**

therefore **dunque, quindi**
they **loro**
thing **cosa**
to think **pensare**
this **questa**
throat **gola**
tie **cravatta**
    bow tie **cravatta a farfalla**
tight **stretto**
time **ora, tempo**
timetable **orario**
tired **stanco**
toast **brindisi** (m)
today **oggi**
together **insieme**
to get together **riunirsi**
tomorrow **domani**
too **anche, troppo**
too many **troppi/e**
too much **troppo/a**
tooth **dente** (m)
torch **torcia**
totally **totalmente**
tour **escursione** (f)
tourism **turismo**
touristic **turistico**
towards **verso, in direzione di**
tower **torre** (f)
town **città**
town hall **municipio**
traditional **tradizionale**
traffic lights **semaforo** (sing)
to train **allenarsi**
train **treno**
trainer **allenatore** (m)
transport **trasporti** (m pl)
to travel **viaggiare**
treasure **tesoro**
to treat **trattare**
treatment **trattamento**
tree **albero**
trousers **pantalone** (m sing)
true **vero**
truly **veramente**
to try on **provare**
Turkey **Turchia**
to turn **girare**
twin beds **letti gemelli**
type **tipo**

U

ugly **brutto**
UK **Regno Unito**
uncle **zio**
under(neath) **sotto**
to understand **capire**
underwater **subacqueo**
unfortunately **purtroppo,
sfortunatamente**
university **università**
unpleasant *(person)*
antipatico
unrepeatable **irripetibile**
until **fino a**
up **su**
us **noi, ci**
USA **Stati Uniti** (m pl)
to use **usare**
useful **utile**
usual **solito**
usually **di solito**
utility room **bagno di
servizio**

V

validity **validità**
value **valore** (m)
various **vario**
vegetable **verdura**
version **versione** (f)
very **molto**
victory **vittoria**
view **vista, panorama** (m)
village **paese** (m), **paesino**
vinegar **aceto**
vineyard **vigna, vigneto**
violet **viola**
virgin **vergine** (f)
to visit **visitare**
volleyball **pallavolo**

W

waist **vita**
waistcoat **gilet** (m)
waiter **cameriere**
waitress **cameriera**
to wake up **svegliarsi**
Wales **Galles** (m)
to walk **camminare,
passeggiare**
walking boots **scarponcini
da trekking**
wall **muro**

wallet **portafogli(o)** (m)
walnut **noce** (f)
to want **desiderare, volere**
war **guerra**
wardrobe **armadio**
to wash **lavare**
washable **lavabile**
washing machine
lavatrice (f)
to watch **guardare**
water **acqua**
way **modo**
we **noi**
wealth **ricchezza**
to wear **indossare, portare**
weather **tempo**
    weather forecast
    previsioni meteo (fpl)
wedding **matrimonio**
week **settimana**
weekly **settimanale**
weight **peso**
    to lose weight **dimagrire**
well **allora, bene**
well-being **benessere** (m)
west **ovest** (m)
what? **(che) cosa?**
when(?) **quando(?)**
where(?) **dove(?)**
which **che**
which? **quale?**
white **bianco**
who, whom **che**
who? **chi?**
why? **perché?**
widow(er) **vedova/o**
width **larghezza**
wife **moglie**
willingly **volentieri**
to win **vincere** (pp **vinto**)
wind **vento**
window **finestra**
wine **vino**
winner **vincitore/trice**
(m/f)
winter **inverno, invernale**
(adj)
to wish **augurare**
wish **augurio**
with **con**
to withdraw *(cash)*
prelevare
without **senza**
woman **donna**

wonderful **meraviglioso**
wonderfully **a meraviglia**
wool **lana**
to work **lavorare**
work **lavoro**
world **mondo, mondiale**
(adj)
wrist **polso**
to write **scrivere** (pp
scritto)

Y

year **anno**
yellow **giallo**
yes **sì**
yesterday **ieri**
you **tu, lei, voi**
young **giovane**
your **tuo, suo, vostro**
youth **giovinezza**

Z

zip **cerniera**